If You Only Knew What You Already Know

Paul Wedding

Harmonie Park Press
Sterling Heights, Michigan • 2008

Printed and bound in the United States of America
Published by
Harmonie Park Press
Liberty Professional Center
35675 Mound Road
Sterling Heights, Michigan 48310-4727
www.harmonieparkpress.com

Publisher: Elaine Gorzelski
Editors: David R. Gorzelski and Karen P. Simmons
Jacket Design: Mitchell Groters
Jacket Photograph: Brian McElhone
Book Design and Typographer: Colleen McRorie

Library of Congress Cataloging-in-Publication Data

Wedding, Paul.
    If you only knew what you already know / [Paul Wedding ; editors, David R.
Gorzelski and Karen P. Simmons].
        p. cm.
    ISBN 0-89990-142-5 (alk. paper)
    1. Spirituality—Miscellanea. 2. Spiritual life—Christianity. 3. Christian
life. I. Gorzelski, David R. II. Simmons, Karen P. III. Title.
    BV4501.3.W398 2008
    204'.4—dc22
                                                    2008033185

To Cindy Allard,
I Love You

Contents

Contents

Acknowledgements

You have come to find what you already have.
—BUDDIST APHORISM

I have been richly blessed to have so many souls assist me through this process. I have been at times undeserving of your unselfish efforts. God only knows how many of you have been here throughout the journey. If you went unnamed you are certainly not forgotten and always in my heart.

I want to thank God for my life, for my past, and for what is to follow. I want to thank my family, especially Michael and Julie Cianciolo. I want to thank Karen MacGaughey for her selfless dedication and belief, especially when I was losing mine. Finally, I would like to thank Harmonie Park Press for believing in me and my work.

I am living proof that when the time is right, God will put the people you need in your life, and place them where they are needed most. It is important to realize that we can all get what we want from life, if we just take the time to help others get what they want.

Thanks to all of you.

◌

Introduction

As we began the final stages of the editing process, this book was sent into the hands of my peers to get their thoughts and opinions on the content. The time had come to start writing the introduction and I was wondering how I could possibly break down the entire contents of this book into a brief description.

Unfortunately the answer came when my sister Julie had to put her five-year-old dog "Rosie" to sleep because of cancer. It was a grueling decision and the family was devastated by the news. Julie shared with me an entry she wrote in her journal later that evening that goes to the heart of my message. She wrote:

> *God I miss Rosie. Death is such a horrible thing for the survivors and there seems to be some truth to the old adage, "no pain no gain." There must be a heaven and our gain in the end is to be reunited with our loved ones. What a masterful plan put forth by God—it's amazing what kind of perspective you gain after a loss. Then when you are reunited with them back again in heaven, you realize that your love was really all that was important—that's what makes heaven, heaven.*

*Could I possibly imagine anything better than a day re-
united with my Grandma, or Grandpa, my aunts, uncles,
friends and Rosie? Nothing could make me happier.
I would be given back what was taken and what truly
mattered. I would be so grateful and grateful people always
act in a way God asks us to. This is how God makes us
perfect. I understand and now appreciate this lesson no
matter how painful. This is what will inspire me to do well
on earth—the promise to be together again with loved ones.
It's rather simple—heaven isn't some magical place—it's
just us living a life of lessons learned—which I guess is
pretty magical stuff after all. Heaven is a place where
everyone cares only about love.*

Although suffering through a tragic loss, my sister had it right.
It is not about learning anything new, just returning to our spiritual
selves, and that is the foundation of what this book is all about.

The Discovery

Over the years I have found that children have a far greater awareness
of God than adults do. There are credible accounts where children
were able to remember the time with our Creator prior to entering the
world and their physical existence. Christ even referred to this event
when he said, "Except ye be converted and become as little children,
ye shall not enter into the Kingdom of Heaven" (Matthew 18:3).

In this passage the word *converted* is very revealing, suggesting
that at a very early age we move away from our natural state of being

and into a consciousness, which takes on a state of duality. This natural state and the prevalent place I write about will be a topic I refer to frequently in this book.

It is my contention that each and every one of us has a competition taking place inside of us. It is a battle waged between two opposing forces. I am not speaking about some dark force competing with God for our soul. What I am referring to is the free will we have been given to make our own decisions and choices.

The competition is the struggle between our ego and spirit, and the one we give the most credence to will be the one we ultimately end up following. This decision will shape our world view based on the teachings we decide are best for us. Because of the consequences, this decision between ego and spirit is simply the most important decision you will ever make.

This decision has nothing to do with the spouse you choose, the career path you go down, the college you end up sending your kids to, or the house you decide to live in. It is about choosing peace and happiness or chaos and unrest.

We are all in a constant state of recall, being summoned to remember and transcend beyond the false self to return to our spiritual beginnings. We are continually called back while in these vessels we call our bodies.

Shedding the ego means returning. ***If You Only Knew What You Already Know*** tells us we have the awareness to return. For whatever the reasons, we choose not to live our lives based on this awareness even though we have demonstrated this knowledge in the past. Returning is the only way if we are going to live a spiritual existence.

I was once told by a psychologist that only 3–5 percent of the people who seek treatment actually change their behavior; this is one of the few things this social science says that I actually believe. People do not change behavior—people return, and it is this conversion that Christ talked about earlier. Unity replaces division and love overrules hatred. This is the place we came from—a state of grace. It is here where people proclaim they have found God, even though God was never missing.

When we return, we again discover that God is God and we are not. When we return, we understand what our place is, what our function is, and what our intended purpose is. It is up to each and every one of us to shed belief systems that no longer make sense. It is up to each and every one of us to see oneness rather than separation.

The Journey

This book has taken three long years to write. My story is true and verifiable. It was written while living in a dumpster in California, a family member's garage, the local jail, and ultimately finished in the home in which I now live. During this journey I received a life sentence, which I am happy to serve. My punishment: Teaching and championing a return to our spiritual selves.

The reason I wrote this book is simple—God wanted me to. He told me I needed to. My name appears as author, but I am nothing more then an outlet. I believe God has written many books that speak of a better way to live life—they just never got into the precious hands of the person holding it at this second.

You are going to read a story of what happens when we allow God to lead, and put our false ideas of life away for good. I truly believe my story would not be uncommon if we only trusted in the power which created us, rather than the counterfeit image we have of who we believe we are. This tussle is a constant struggle in all of our lives.

Marian Wright Edelman said, "Service is the rent we pay to be living. It is the very purpose of life and not something you do in your spare time." Purpose is what gives our lives true meaning. It is my contention we are here to serve each other, love each other, and care for each other—the rest is just semantics. *To love one another* are words spoken from the highest of authorities.

One thing I can promise is this—whatever your expectations are in life, they are only going to be met based on how you think and act. If you think about it, life is really about remembering and not learning anything new—***If You Only Knew What You Already Know***. Returning is the key and the only authentic freedom is the freedom from ego. Everything else is merely an illusion.

Keep the peace, and God Bless
Paul Wedding

❦

Long Road Out

We cannot treat others as if they were a paper towel,
simply pulling one off to clean up the messes of life,
only to discard and pull another. The roll is only so long.
—PAUL J. WEDDING

Recently I watched a documentary on cable television about natural disasters. The show focused on tidal waves, hurricanes, wild-fires, and tornados. When you witness one of these disasters in motion, you realize just how small and powerless you are in the face of nature. What a horrific sight to see, all of that beautiful landscape destroyed in a matter of minutes, and people left homeless among pure devastation.

I was trying to imagine how something which took years to create could be destroyed so quickly and use this example as a meta-phor for a large part of my life. Other human beings represented the landscape, the flowers, and the trees—these people represented all that was beautiful. As I entered their lives, I was the equivalent of a human natural disaster. As I exited their lives, I would leave in a way that left them far worse off than they were prior to the storm hitting.

What I destroyed took years to rebuild: trust, self-worth, and the ability to give and receive love. During this dark period of my life, which spanned quite a few years, I had very little respect for others. People represented nothing more than pawns in my game of life. My only thoughts were: "What will you do for me?" and "What can I get out of you?"

My Specialty

One of the "gifts" that I was told I possessed was the ability to sell. What I sold, and what people bought, was my deception about what I was telling them. I often said, "Your feelings and desires are safe with me"; "You can trust me with confidence"; and, of course, "I am the man who will love you forever."

The fact was, I never cared one lick about any facet of their lives or the challenges they faced. The same challenges I promised to meet head on with them never mattered. I did not care about one damn thing as it related to anything else. It was simply *all about me.*

Making My "Mark"

The truth was, I was a con man, thief, cheat, and a liar. I was incredibly good at what I did. I had what any good con needed: no feelings or empathy for the "mark," completely guiltless for any pain I caused. A con man can charm you with words of grandeur in one breath and steal you blind in the next.

Compassion was a word I could not spell, let alone offer to someone else. How can you give away something that you yourself do not have? Every person I had any relationship with during this dark period was left cheated, depleted financially, and left emotionally bankrupt.

If God Almighty were to have lent me twenty dollars, He would never have seen it again—it was a game for me. When my own father loaned me money, he would always say to me, "Don't forget where you got it." I never forgot; I only "forgot" to give it back. I took money to pay off gambling debts and to wine and dine other "marks." Whatever I wanted—I got. If I wanted something, but didn't have the money, I would "borrow" without guilt. If I could not borrow the money, I would steal.

Three's a Crowd

There was one instance when I borrowed my girlfriend's car, along with some of her money, in order to drive to the home of another woman for a night of dinner and a concert. The following morning my girlfriend confronted me as to where I was the night before; I was supposed to be at a twelve-step program for gamblers. Seems her girlfriend was at the same concert and saw me with this other woman. I admitted that I was at the concert and with another woman. My girlfriend then asked, "How could you do this to me?" I answered back, "This was your fault—you screwed up and trusted me!"

When I was not working a "mark," I would live in my mother's house; when not living there, I lived on the street. Far too often my family would hear about the pain and anguish I was causing and urged me to seek professional help.

What's Up, Doc?

Psychology can be your ally in these dark moments. A doctor I went to diagnosed me as having a condition known as bipolar disorder (manic depression). In my family, the word depression was recited about as often as "please pass the salt." The doctor told me this was the reason I was behaving this way, and my behavior was blamed on whichever state of the disorder I was experiencing. Forty-five minutes later, the doctor prescribed a bottle of pills and told me to come back for another appointment.

I was just given a professional excuse for being the way I was, and I had a bottle of pills to prove it. The last thing you want to give a person like me is an excuse and a reason to believe I am not responsible for the actions I have chosen.

Our society has become overly medicated. There is a commercial for a pill if you're experiencing restless leg syndrome, and one of the side effects is an increased urge to gamble. There is another pill for depression that has suicide as a possible side effect. What I knew for certain was that no pill was going to have any positive effect on me.

As I took the medication and visited the doctor, the only thing that changed was the dosage. I was still the human natural disaster, devastating all those around me and treating them with little or no respect. I am certain that some people need these medications just

4

to get through the day. Please understand that I am not indicting all who take meds, only what it meant to me and my situation.

For me, my diagnosis was simple—I was a roué, an impassible human being. The only thing that could possibly have had any effect on me was losing what I needed to control. When you live in states of low source energy or darkened states, you never experience suffering; you also never experience joy, compassion or happiness of any kind. You're breathing, but you only exist.

A New Group of Friends

One evening last year I was speaking at a function in Michigan. The building was rather large, with an area for me to go and prepare some final thoughts. A loud commotion coming from the end of the hall caught my attention. I walked down to the room; there were a few hundred people seated around tables, ten to a table.

The person leading the group came up to me and said, "Hello, are you here for the meeting?" I replied that I was not; I was here presenting a lecture. "What is your presentation on?" he asked. I told him that I was going to speak on the Power of Belief. "Is it open to the public?" "It is," I replied. He then asked if his group could come in and listen, at which point I invited the group into the auditorium where I was speaking.

During my lecture, I learned the group was there for a Narcotics Anonymous (NA) meeting. Afterwards, I spoke with many of them individually, and the one thing I remember is how each person was able to recite back to me the last date they had abused a narcotic.

This is the effect of what a spiritually transcending experience has on us; the experience is indelibly stamped in our hearts and minds. The immediate impact of these types of experience tells us life will never again be the same.

Turning Point

One of these experiences happened to me on April 19, 2003. This particular day started out like most others did. I remember turning on the television around noon and flipping mindlessly through the channels. After a short while I went into the kitchen to grab a bite to eat—the time was 12:37 in the afternoon.

As I stood in the kitchen, a presence came through me; it was unlike anything I had ever experienced before. This presence had no voice, nor was it some religious conversion taking place, just a message that clearly detailed for me the new direction my life was going to move in. There was no explanation how it was going to happen or when I could expect it. There were two things I knew at that moment to be certain—one, it was not the medication; two, it was not my imagination.

There were tears, laughter, excitement, and a feeling of the world being lifted off my shoulders! "Hello, God, is that you?" For someone who wandered each day oblivious to anyone or anything, why on Earth would God be talking to me? More ridiculous than that idea was what I believed my instructions to be. "God," I said, "this is Paul Wedding you are bothering, and what You are asking me is to do is perform a task nonexistent in my DNA. I am certain

You reached the wrong person, so check the number and try again. Thanks for dropping by anyway, and if it is not too much trouble, while You are here, could you leave me a fifty?"

Time for a Change

Whenever some type of miraculous event takes place, a new technology is developed, or some cure is discovered, we always attach the act to human ingenuity, not divine intervention. If the proof of God's hand is not there, or things cannot be explained, we call it a coincidence, chance, or just plain luck.

Everyday there are stories of miracles, examples of the championing of the human spirit that transpire all over the world, where eyes are opened and hearts swell. We usually learn of such events during the last fifteen or twenty seconds of the evening news, following the thirty minutes of chaos, hatred, and violence.

The good you see is God; the rest comes from us, the "intelligent" human being. We go with what we know, even though there is something far greater available to every one of us. We are capable of transcending to a place of peace and happiness, if we would only surrender. Ego consciousness is not in the business of surrender.

I remember a pastor once telling me that when God calls us to a purpose, if we fail to act, God will pass this purpose on to someone else. Not long after my experience, I found surrender was the only option that fit me. Being called to a higher awareness was not only how I wanted to live my life, I also wanted to share it with everyone. Identifying the blind spot of those who trusted me, then exploiting it for my selfish agenda is a painful reminder of what happens when we live through ego; the good news is that the grace of God is available to all of us!

Lost and Found

My transformation was not in front of an altar; it was a direct experience with the Almighty. This means putting your faith in the power that created you, trusting in that power and accepting that what you are doing in life is right, and walking a path resistant to fear. I hear a lot of people proclaim that they have found God! My response is, how can you find something that was never lost or missing?

God is not some complicated mathematical equation on a blackboard, or found in a scientific test. God is found in the deepest recesses of your heart. *If You Only Knew What You Already Know* tells us there is nothing to learn, simply return. Ego tells us we are separate; the further we get away from our natural state, the more we attract the negative experiences of life. The way back is met through disconnecting from what we have been taught, and letting go of what others have led us to believe.

Finally, we can reconnect to what we already know but fail to do for a variety of reasons, and these topics will be addressed in the following chapters. From the second we formed thought, a process called conditioning was put into motion by the people who knew what was best for us. Their motives were more than likely pure, intending to use their experiences of life as a template to lead us into our teens, and eventually into adulthood.

What you will discover is that all the data we processed as truth becomes our burden to dismantle later in our lives. Returning to our natural state does not make us immune from troubling situations, or give us a "get out of pain free" card. What it promises is a very effective way as to how these situations affect you and how you finally handle them. What I have discovered is that as humans we are confronted with events that knock us off our axis. The idea *I know what is best* is the greatest destruction of the intellect.

Not Everyone Buys into It

I have always been open with others about my life prior to the shift. Some applaud the transformation while others believe it to be insincere, but I really do not care either way. My openness with my then-wife caused a great deal of anxiety for her, unsure if my love was true or if she was just another "mark." She went to a psychologist with my storied past, and based on a forty-five minute evaluation came out with an assessment that people may wish to change, but statistics tell us that only 3–5 percent ever do. She was then given the names of three attorneys for the purpose of dissolving our marriage.

I have asked the question, "If human beings have such a low rate of changing negative behavior into productive behavior, why is the science of therapy needed?" I was once told that if you are going to bet on a horse, judge your wager on the past, and boy-oh-boy do we judge people on their past, forgetting we have one as well.

When it comes to people not changing, I am in total agreement; we really do not change. What causes someone to be different is returning to the spiritual existence from which we were all created; created in the image that only knows grace, love, and kindness.

I can tell you from personal experience that life can be a living hell; I have done things in my life that would cause others to see me as the anti-Christ, a sociopath who is unfixable. I have not only lived in the finest of homes, but also slept with rats in dumpsters. I can relate to just about any story out there.

When we believe in living our lives through our ego, the road is very long. When we choose to reconnect with God, the trip back will be no more complicated than going to the mailbox. So take my hand and I will take yours, and through the rest of these chapters **we will walk this path together.**

∂

Making the Case for God

You live in this world, but are not of this world.
— JESUS CHRIST (JOHN 17:11–14)

I find the boomerang to be a very unique tool. It is the only instrument I know of that returns once it is released—that is its sole purpose— to return back to the originating source. The boomerang was first used over twenty thousand years ago and continues to be in use today in many different capacities—from competitive sporting events to hunting. The Australian Aborigines use the boomerang to test their skills in hand-to-hand combat, as well as a weapon for catching food.

Our lives here on Earth resemble that of the boomerang, with the goal of returning to the hand that released us into the universe. Whatever our thinking has led us to believe; ultimately, we are going to return. The quote from Jesus is very revealing. "You live in this world, but are not of this world" suggests we all originated from another place. We are all indeed spiritual beings having a *human* experience rather than human beings having a *spiritual* experience.

What I am writing about is not returning to our spiritual self simply through the act of death, but rather going back while we are still alive and in our present form. Each and every one of us is connected in this universe. We have all been created in the image of God, unique in our creation, but in the grand scheme of things just a small branch on the tree of humanity. When you think about God, think about the way God thinks, the way God acts, and the qualities God possesses. Now take a good look at the world we live in; it is not a very congruent picture, is it? We are living in very tumultuous times, to be certain. Whenever we allow ego to make decisions for us, bad times are not very far away.

We are on Earth for a very short time. If you were to measure eternity against your walk on this planet, the sum of time would be so small it would be incalculable. With that in mind, what is the reason God put us here? What is our purpose, the defining function for us being here? Asking ourselves, or anyone else for that matter, the question of "why," never seems to bring about a clear answer. Only fate will be able to answer that question for us one day. The truth is we all know the answer to that question, but very few people—those who think from their spiritual self, instead of their ego, understand the answer.

Assembly Required

When I purchase products that require assembly, here is how I usually go about the process of putting it together. I open the box, lay all the pieces on the floor, empty out the hardware, and then begin to look for the quickest way to assemble the product. It's basically the way every guy tackles a project. Look at the pieces and try to make them fit the best way you can—no direction, no instruction.

What happens is that we keep trying to do things our own way, when right there in front of us is something that could have made the job so much easier—the manual. Anytime something begins to drift away from where it belongs, the chances of that object returning to the source becomes more remote as time passes on—pretty simple logic really.

If a raft begins to float away from a dock, chances of retrieving it grow smaller and smaller by the second. Because of the movement of the water, the raft will need to be pulled back by another source. This is much the same when it comes to our relationship with God. When we choose to act through ego, we behave in ways that move us further and further away from God—usually because the path we decided on is *our* way—not the spiritual one.

The Scripture shows six things that God hates. One of the six is division among His people. Division is the direct opposite of unity, which is the goal I believe God had in mind. Who are God's people? Who does this include? Is it the people of Rhode Island? Those who live on the Upper East Side of Manhattan? I don't know; do God's people live only in Russia? Of course not! God's people are found at every corner, in every nook and cranny of this planet. We are all the same people coming from the same Creator.

A Personal Invitation

Recently I received an invitation in the mail to attend a four-part seminar entitled "Does It Matter?" The seminar was going to tackle five important questions:

1. Does what we believe in actually make sense?
2. What gives life meaning?
3. Do all religions lead to the same place?
4. Can man live without God?
5. Why is there so much evil in the world?

Well, I would like to answer each of these questions objectively.

Does What We Believe in Actually Make Sense?

The problem with this question is in how it is asked. I think it would sound better if it was asked "Does what *you* believe in actually make sense?" Because *we* do not all think the same. As strident as we are to impose our beliefs and ideals down the throats of others, it is difficult to move someone off of their own beliefs and ideals with much success.

The drive to push people off of their beliefs is especially reprehensible when dealing with an individual's belief in God. God has given us all free will, the ability to think separately, and an ability to decide what does and does not make sense as part of that free will.

What makes sense for me may not ring true with you. This approach should never lead to anyone trying to convince another that their beliefs are wrong, especially in topics that can be considered subjective. We all need to practice understanding, patience, and respect of others without judgment—steps God would want us to engage in.

Too often we think from the ego, the part of us that needs to be right. The right way is a more spiritual approach—one of grace, which is an act of returning. I have some close friends of the Hindu faith; a faith that lends itself to a very spiritual way of approaching life, living in a peaceful and compassionate manner. They suffer a lot of indignities and abuse from those claiming to be religious, although I do not think this is what God had in mind.

Their beliefs differ from mine and vice versa, but we understand and appreciate each other based on love and respect—even if we do not think the same. By returning to the state of love, you shed the ego, thus opening the door to oneness rather than division.

What Gives Life Meaning?

What gives life meaning comes from the inside. There is very little the external world can offer us in terms of giving meaning to life. When your idea is that the true meaning of life is derived through the tangible, you are setting yourself up for major disappointment. Tangible goods will never be enough and ultimately will never suffice. The need for a bigger home, nicer automobile, and other tangible objects only works to soothe the ego.

Once you get wrapped up in this trap, it is difficult to return to your spiritual self. Your external identification becomes tied to things, and in this place life becomes a never-ending pursuit; a pursuit which does not give our lives meaning.

It is my contention that the meaning of life is all about having a purpose. When we align ourselves with God, we align with a purpose as well. There is nothing worse than the feeling of being useless, feeling that we are simply floating aimlessly from one day to the next. We can all get the things in life we desire most when we help others to also get the things *they* desire most.

There is a song I once heard on the radio by the rock group Nickelback. There is a verse in the song that talks about purpose and what could result through cooperation instead of conflict.

It went

> *If everyone cared and nobody cried*
> *If everyone loved and nobody lied*
> *If everyone shared and swallowed their pride*
> *We'd see the day when nobody died.*

These are very simple words with an incredibly powerful meaning. Each line begins with "If everyone"; we are all one, united from the beginning. Compelling purpose, as a basis for a meaningful life, will bring all the feelings associated with a meaningful existence—love, happiness, kindness, and compassion.

Do All Religions Lead to the Same Place?

I was listening to a pastor that I know and respect a great deal. He said that religion is facing challenges that it has never had to face before. I think the challenges the pastor was eluding to are the changing attitudes people have towards religion. I do not know for certain if all religions lead to the same place, but all divisions do, and I believe that is what religion does best—promotes division.

In 2005, I wrote a weekly column for a newspaper. One of the columns I wrote dealt with us having a direct relationship with God. I began this column with a quote, as I did all my columns. The quote was made by a man I admire a great deal, Dr. Carl Jung, a Swiss-born psychiatrist. He said, "One of the main functions of formalized religion is to protect people against a direct experience of God." His point seems pretty clear to me: religion would have you believe that the only way to God is through the church.

Attempting to force people to believe that your way is the only way will only create more resentment in the minds of those who choose to exercise free will. The mentality of people who force others to follow a dogma as salvation will ultimately backfire. Believing that God does not love people who choose a different path is division in the making.

Let me give you an example. My wish is to hit a golf ball with power and accuracy, so here are my options. I can watch the professionals on television for hours at a time, watch golf videos, listen to instructors, or read magazines to try and accomplish this goal. This is instruction *without action*. Without the direct experience of actually hitting the golf ball, what is ultimately accomplished? Nothing. You must have that direct experience of hitting the ball yourself, free of outside intervention. You gain clarity by trusting in what you are feeling and experiencing things firsthand.

Can Man Live without God?

Following a major scientific breakthrough, three scientists asked God if they could meet with Him, and God agreed. The lead scientist told

God of yet another breakthrough that he and his colleagues were responsible for discovering. He went on to tell God of the amazing strides science deserves the credit for, one of which was the process of cloning, a way to duplicate human beings.

The scientist said, "The point I am trying to make to You, God, is that we really do not need You anymore, we can take over from here, so thanks for all Your help, we got it handled." God thought about it briefly, and then responded, "You do not need Me anymore? O.K., that is fine, and by the way, you'll be on your own to find soil, water, sun, and food."

Our planet is crumbling spiritually at an alarming rate and that is on us—not God. Can we live day in and day out without God in our lives? I think the answer is pretty apparent—we cannot, nor should we try. We can certainly live without the false representations people put forth about God, but not without His grace.

Why Is There So Much Evil in the World?

In the book of Genesis, the first thirty-two verses are about what God said and what he created. Verse 31 reads: "God saw all that He had made, and it was very good. And there was evening, and there was morning—sixth day." Now if God created all that is very good, then why are we living in a world directly opposite from this?

To me, that answer is very simple: the problem is *hatred.* Is there an easy explanation as to why hatred rules the heart and minds of so many? Well, that depends on where you go for clarification. You can look to some force of evil that is in constant competition with the Almighty for your soul, or you can look at what happens when we believe in our separation from God and other people.

The latter of the two make more sense to me. How can there be a force greater than that from which we emanated? Our demise will not be fire or brimstone or some incredible period of torment. We are creating the hostility that will lead to the end.

Where Did All the Dinosaurs Go?

There was an article written in a syndicated magazine some time ago entitled "Marching Toward Extinction." The article went on to give one theory as to what happened to the dinosaur. It claimed that the dinosaurs' demise came about due to its inability to adapt. It could not keep up with the changes taking place all around it.

The human species is heading down that same path. Our ability to adapt depends on our ability to change the way we handle conflict, people, and most importantly, our egos. The only way to solve this problem is to return back to that state I keep talking about. It is all about developing an ability to practice, and then display, spiritual principles. If we do not, or refuse to, we as well will become extinct.

We are not learning if we are not returning. The evidence to back this statement up can be seen daily just by looking at the world we live in, and what we have created all in the name of God—the same God who knows only love, peace, patience, forgiveness, and grace. It is maddening to see our man-made performance of the interpretation of these basic and beautiful blueprints for living a spiritual life—a life of meaning and substance.

So what are the answers to combat ego, greed, and hatred? I believe a good place to start is to retrace our steps all the way back to the beginning. *Making a Case for God* means living by HIS blueprint, word for word, and without qualification. It means exercising free will, asking questions without fear of verbal retaliation. It means to "love each other as I have loved you."

⌘

They Are Not Synonymous

Going to church does not make you a Christian
any more than going to the garage makes you a car.
—LAURENCE J. PETER (1919–88)
U.S. EDUCATOR AND WRITER

When two words are said to be synonymous, it is because those words are exact or very close in meaning. Spirituality and religion share some common themes; to say they are synonymous is not accurate. Religion gives answers to people; it also carries a tenet of dogma one must strictly follow to be considered part of the group.

Spirituality, I believe, lost its true meaning when man turned it into a religion, rather than a way to live your life. I was near completion in writing this book when I received a telephone call from a radio station. The person asked if I would like the opportunity to come on the air, as kind of a pre-release interview.

Without hesitation I jumped at the chance, believing this to be a wonderful avenue to get the word out on my new book. I was told they had a dedicated listening audience, and the host, known for his longevity in the radio business, assured me I would be interviewed by a true professional. After being assigned a time and date, I was asked, "How long have you been writing religious material?" Without hesitation I responded, "Well, in all honesty, my writing has nothing to do with religion."

I have had similar experiences in the past following my lectures. Attendees will occasionally come up to me and ask when I speak on spirituality, am I in effect speaking about religion?

In the Name of God

I believe that spirituality and religion are closely related in the minds of most people because of their strong connection to God—but that is where I believe the similarities end. Spirituality asks redeeming questions. Spiritual qualities are things like love, kindness, honesty, understanding, humility, and a life free of judgments.

I am constantly amazed at the different ways people have come to experience and understand the Creator of this universe. Some portray God as a bloodthirsty tyrant who keeps records of every one of our sins and doles out punishment during the final judgment. Others view God as one who is full of unconditional love, grace, mercy, patience, and forgiveness.

For the purpose of writing this chapter, I visited several different places of worship including temples, churches, fellowships, and kingdom halls. There are no "good" places or "bad" places I visited. I believe the way any individual chooses to worship is a private decision that deserves to be respected without condemnation.

I wanted to experience as many different services as I could and see what developed out of each experience. I came away from each visit with an opinion. An opinion based on observation and participation.

Tragically, what I discovered by attending the array of services was the influence on people by leaders to make sure their *flock* was surrounded with like-minded thinkers—the classic version of the pack mentality.

I Believe

I believe religion can restore hope to a soul who feels hopeless, and faith to a soul who feels there is nothing worthy to trust in. I have been told numerous times of stories or "testimonials" by people who have had what they called a "religious experience." It seems to me that a large number of these experiences occurred during a period of time when life had them by the throat, asphyxiated in the grip of their most difficult moments.

Abusive relationships, gambling, drugs, pornography, and other addictive behaviors can saddle us with excessive amounts of guilt and shame. These people end up seeing their lives as hopeless, useless, and not worthy of love.

For a variety of reasons these souls, *through a chosen destructive path,* are unable to find the door to liberation. Although many turn to professionals for help, many times it is religion that saves them from committing threatening acts to themselves or others; in short, religion offers freedom where professionals and psychologists have failed.

Just Visiting

A few years back I was invited to a fellowship in Windsor, Ontario. Their catch phrase was, "Living Life Inside Out." By now you understand that I am a person who believes in living from the internal self; the mind-body-spirit connection is very important to me.

"Living Life Inside Out" certainly sounded good, so I was happy to attend. The service I went to was anything but spiritual or uplifting. In retrospect, it was downright frightening! One thing that disturbs me is when a church calls their organization a house of God and says that all are welcome to attend, but in reality this is not always the case.

Welcome to attend, in this case, was really determined by lifestyle, sacrifice, and the level of ability to conform. We are all creations of our Creator, unique in design, yet spiritually connected.

Great Lakes State

I live in the state of Michigan. One of the wonderful things about living in this state is experiencing the four seasons. I can certainly live without the never-ending winter months, but this comes with the territory.

Spring is the season where everything comes alive. The lush green grass, cascade of blooming flowers, and array of foraging wildlife are all available for us to take in and appreciate. I use this season for opening the swimming pool and working in my backyard. I enjoy arranging my yard into a sanctuary, a place to sit and observe the magnificence of what God has provided for my pleasure to enjoy and cherish.

I have a neighbor who drifts over on occasion and we will sit and talk, enjoying the scenery. One afternoon, he was complimenting me on how beautiful everything in the yard looked and then offered a suggestion as to how it could be improved. I asked him how. He said to me, "It would really be nice if we could just eliminate all the squirrels."

I was a little taken aback by his comments. He continued by saying, "These rodents come into my backyard and destroy everything I work so hard to create. These squirrels are just an intolerable nuisance." I quietly disagreed and thought to myself that as one of God's creatures, squirrels can actually be quite amusing and entertaining.

There are some religions that view other people as the squirrel in the backyard. They are intolerant and judgmental to those coming from a different perspective. These are the people *digging holes in the manicured lawn of their undeniable truths*, but truth does not ring the same in every mind. When intolerance gives way to seeing things through a benevolent eye, the ball game always changes.

Back to the Church

The two pastors in the church I was visiting in Windsor did a lot of yelling and screaming, speaking passionately about hell, blood, and burnt offerings. Pointing towards the front door, they spoke to their congregation in terms of *us* against *them*, the *good* Christians against the *bad* Christians, the bad ones being those who did not subscribe to the exact tenets of their beliefs.

Not only did they tell their flock how to live their lives, they wanted to tell complete strangers, or in my case visitors, how to do it as well. When their excessive badgering falls on deaf ears, the response is that you *heathens* will now be traveling mach speed to the furthest point south. If they were unable to change you and your beliefs, they would simply treat you as the enemy.

I once saw a television commercial for an online mortgage business that would bring different lenders together, allowing the buyer the best rate. One by one they made their pitch to the borrowing family; at the end of the commercial you see the family escorting the lenders out the door. Each lender in turn gives one last unconvincing sales pitch to the family as to why they should do business with them.

Religions promote their message in much the same way. The tone clearly implies that their beliefs are the *one and only* way. They preach that the only way for God to love you more is to attend the right church and obey a tenet of beliefs handed down as truth; and, if you *really* want God to be good to you, make sure you do not forget the most important part—*make sure you donate a lot of your money.*

Give 'til It Hurts

Many religions use tithing as a blueprint to redemption. They believe a certain percentage of your income should go into their coffers. Now, *many do use this money for worthy causes;* however, there are some religions where money seems to be the root of all their evils. Watch any preacher take command of the "electric pulpit" and they will preach to you to send money in the hopes of curing every disease known to man. *Money* is the message when you watch these preachers on television with whom you have no personal connection.

I listened to one preacher on television reading a letter from a "sad soul" who had not seen any change in his situation since he started donating. The preacher's solution, of course, was to send more money—it was time to let God *really* know how serious you are.

There is nothing religious about being broke. There is no justifiable reason to send money to the "electric pulpit" if your family is truly suffering. These preachers could not care less about you or your needs. I can promise you that your Creator wants to see your family vibrant and abundant, not broke and living in squalor.

When I think about ministry, I think Jesus Christ. When I think of a "true" healer, I think of Jesus Christ. I have no opinion when it comes to these *faith healers* who extol their beliefs through the television. Maybe they are real, or maybe they are just religious placebos.

Today, religion takes a great deal of credit for bringing people closer to God. In reality, it's spirituality that brings you closer. There are a number of examples: St. Francis of Assisi, Mother Teresa, and Gandhi relinquished all of their material possessions in their life's mission because they were moved spiritually.

Walking the Walk

Christ walked from one village to the next, ministering to anyone who would listen; healing all those who asked. If necessary, he traveled by boat. His attire was a simple robe and sandals, and when he grew tired, he would sleep on the floors of homes in the villages.

Religious healers today advertise which "arena" they will be performing miracles in, coming to each town in a Learjet. As they take the stage they are tailored in Armani suits, and their sleeping quarters always involve five-star hotels. Preying, not praying, on lost souls, these healers appear to have found a way to make a living through a legal form of extortion.

Christ lived a life all of us should try and duplicate every second of every day. If you claim to be a Christian, then live like one. Do your best in every situation, but also realize we think with our ego, not always with our spiritual self. We will not always pass the test, and the key is to catch yourself in those moments. Take a moment to reflect on the simple question reiterated so often today—*What would Jesus do?*

Where Do We Go from Here?

Jesus was once asked, "What is the greatest commandment?" He could have simply responded, "That all the commandments have the same weight." However, he answered "Love the Lord God with all you have, and love thy neighbor as I have loved you." This suggests that the greatest of the commandments is to love one another.

Today, however, many religions fail to teach this; instead, their message is one of separatism, division, and hatred towards those with different beliefs. I often wonder, if Jesus Christ returned for a weekend and looked around and saw all the hatred and division we have created in the name of religion—*would he still declare himself a Christian?*

What has made this world so crazy and full of hatred? The Scriptures speak of six things that God hates. Division among His people is one of the biggies. Today many religions employ division as their national anthem. The teachings we hear from a number of religions today are the antithesis of the language of God—completely opposite of what the true messages were intended to relay.

Jesus said, "No one approaches the Father but through me." He never mentioned religious leaders! God does not condemn those who refuse to conform, or see one person as better than another simply because of religious affiliation. Seeing each of us as the same, and loving each other, is how we honor God. Today we are seeing a trend in this country that has people searching for a better way to nourish their souls. Indeed, there is another way. In the words of Lenny Bruce, "People are straying away from church and going back to God."

~

Teachings of the False Self

The ego is a wrong-minded attempt to perceive yourself as you wish to be,
rather than who you are. `Yet you can know yourself only as you are,
because that is all you can be sure of. Everything else is open to question.
—A COURSE IN MIRACLES

This is a chapter I enjoyed writing very much. Like all of the other principles in this book, there is nothing new to learn. As you read this chapter, please do so with an open mind. Truly give it consideration because what you will find at the end of the day is uncompromised truth. Read some, think some. Read some more, think some more.

God is uncompromising truth and knows everything about us, good and bad. We, on the other hand, think and speak with deception without batting an eye, because we are human and think like a human. When you finish reading this chapter, I hope you will have a clear understanding about who the false self is: how it rents space in your mind, why you release it, and come to our true nature of being.

I want to begin with a story. I tell this story because it goes to the heart and soul of my message. It tells a story of how many have interpreted the magnificent journey of life, of what we think is important, and what we find when we realize how off we have been.

Four Boyfriends

Once upon a time there was a girl who had four boyfriends.

She loved the fourth boyfriend the most and adorned him with rich robes and treated him to the finest of delicacies. She gave him nothing but the best.

She also loved the third boyfriend very much and was always showing him off to neighboring kingdoms. However, she feared that one day he would leave her for another.

She also loved her second boyfriend. He was her confidant and was always kind, considerate, and patient with her. Whenever the girl faced a problem, she could confide in him, and he would help her get through the difficult times.

The girl's first boyfriend was a very loyal partner and had made great contributions in maintaining her wealth and kingdom. However, she did not love the first boyfriend. Although he loved her deeply, she hardly took notice of him.

One day, the girl fell ill and she knew her time was short. She thought of her luxurious life and wondered, "I now have four boyfriends with me, but when I die, I'll be all alone."

Thus, she asked the fourth boyfriend, "I loved you the most, endowed you with the finest clothing and showered great care over you. Now that I am dying, will you follow me and keep me company?"

"No way!" replied the fourth boyfriend and he walked away without another word.

His answer cut like a sharp knife right into her heart.

The sad girl then asked the third boyfriend, "I loved you all my life. Now that I am dying, will you follow me and keep me company?"

"No!" replied the third boyfriend. "Life is too good! When you die, I'm going to marry someone else!"

Her heart sank and turned cold. She then asked the second boyfriend, "I have always turned to you for help and you've always been there for me. When I die, will you follow me and keep me company?"

"I'm sorry, I can't help you this time," replied the second boyfriend. "At the very most, I can only walk with you to your grave."

His answer struck her like a bolt of lightning, and the girl was devastated.

Then a voice called out: "I'll go with you. I'll follow you no matter where you go." The girl looked up, and there was her first boyfriend. He was very skinny, as he suffered from malnutrition and neglect.

Greatly grieved, the girl said, "I should have taken better care of you when I had the chance!"

Divide and Conquer

In truth, you have four boyfriends in your lives:

Your fourth boyfriend is your body. No matter how much time and effort you lavish in making it look good, it will leave you when you die.

Your third boyfriend is your possessions, status and wealth.
When you die, it will all go to others.

Your second boyfriend is your family and friends. No matter
how much they have been there for you, the furthest they can stay
with you is up to the grave.

And your first boyfriend is your soul. It is often neglected
in pursuit of wealth, power, and pleasures of the world. However,
your soul is the only thing that will follow you wherever you go.
Cultivate, strengthen and cherish it now, for it is the only part of
you that will follow you to the throne of God and continue with you
throughout eternity.

This is a great example of the internal struggle we face between
ego and spirit. The ego is the part of us wanting to be at war; it divides
and looks to conquer, no matter the cost. Then there is the spirit,
the part of us that just wants to exist and be at peace. We all deal
on a daily basis with the struggle between these two opposing forces.

When we come into this world, we enter through our parents.
When we are able to form and hold a thought, we give birth as well.
We give life to the ego—this false self I am speaking about. It is the
part that cares the least for the part that cares the most. The ego
has an appetite that will never feel satisfied; it devours attention,
externalism, cynicism, judgments and separation.

When I lecture, I offer this illustration about separation. I will
hold up a glass of milk and ask, "Where did this milk come from?"
Invariably someone would say, "From a cow?" Then I would ask,
"Well which cow?" Usually what I hear is, "Any cow, they are all
the same." Then I will hold up a vial of blood and ask, "Where did

this blood come from?" The answer is usually, "It came from a person." "OK, which person?" And the response usually is, "Well, any person, we are all the same." This idea that we are all the same is an idea for many that is hard to accept. It goes against what we have been led to believe, even when we know this belief is false.

Keeping Up with the Joneses

So what are the things the ego has taught us to take on as truth? The first is how we wish to be identified by others through the things we accumulate, and will continue to accumulate as necessary.

You see, the ego is consumed with being liked and accepted and is willing to go to great lengths to get this approval. The more stuff you have, the nicer things you own, the more people will like you. That is the mentality of the ego.

Do you know anyone that fits this mold? I am willing to bet you probably know more than one. The large home, fast boat, fancy car—all things we don't need, but end up being identified with. Social and volunteer work carry little value in the world of the ego. What we end up being identified by are the THINGS WE HAVE ATTACHED OURSELVES TO.

As we accumulate these things, people around us are accumulating things as well, and the need to gather more and more stuff becomes an obsession. We work more and save less, not wanting anyone to get a leg up on us. The more we pursue this false truth, the further away we drift from the "real" truth and we end up insulating ourselves in a maze leading to nowhere.

What Will My Neighbors Think?

The question must be asked: What happens in the face of an unexpected or unforeseen event that can strike any one of us at any given time? What happens if you are involved in an accident causing long-term hardship and the company you have depended upon is unable to pay your salary and decides to let you go?

This is where we now move into the next aspect of ego. That company that is no longer there to support you, leads us straight into the "what are others going to think of me," part of the program. Because ego is a fear-based belief, we panic at the idea of losing our status. If we lose our job because of some unforeseen event, assets we have accumulated must now be liquidated. This liquidation turns into a loss of identity, the loss of who we are—and the loss of our false self.

I know a few individuals who work out at the same fitness center as I do, and their only form of identity is their muscular physique. When you see them out in the real world they are like the proverbial fish out of water. When we attach ourselves to the things we believe solidify us as human beings, we set ourselves up for failure—attachments never last over the long haul.

It Is Ours for Only a Short Time

At some point in our lives, those things we believe we cannot live without will no longer be ours. We need to see things as things and in no way a part of our significance. The next teaching and probably most dangerous teaching of all is the false belief in separation.

Separation goes completely against any spiritual principle, because spirit is truth and ego is false.

The only truth in separation is the false belief in the existence of it. It was once said, "No man is an island" and this is true, because nothing can be accomplished without the help of others. Like the example I used earlier in this chapter, the point is we are all the same, and come from the same place—there is no denying that fact. In the Scriptures it says among the things that God hates the most is division among His people. One absolute truth is we are all God's people.

We believe in separation based on skin, height, weight, abilities, affluence, age, to where you were born. This is also classic ego, because the ego was born out of separation. Religious leaders talk about separation based on dogma, politicians based on party lines and hate groups based on whatever it is they believe in—but it is all false! The only truth is oneness, the oneness the Creator sees; the Creator who makes the sun rise and set everyday.

I do not have to waste your time by giving you countless examples of what happens when ego overrules spirit—the results are painfully obvious. My definition for ego is—Edging God Out. We are drifting further and further away from God, so far away in fact, that the only way back to our true self may be impossible if we continue to believe in what we know to be false.

Crying for Attention

When my daughter Jennifer was a young child she loved getting into the cupboard underneath the sink in the bathroom. I am not sure if it was the colors of the bottles that attracted her, but she was always after the cleaning agents we stored there. I would stand and watch and when she got her mitts on one of the bottles, she would look up at me and smile.

I would bend down and we began jostling back and forth over the bottle, and soon enough I would take it away from her. Jennifer would begin to cry and pound her hands on her knees; eventually, she would leave and find something else less threatening to occupy her time.

What Jennifer wanted to have more than anything was what I had taken away, and it is also the thing that would have caused her the greatest amount of harm. This is much the same with ego. We will kick and scream all the way until the end thinking what we believe is usually the most important. Our egos are what will cause us the greatest harm, but like a child we do not understand this and will scream and shout until we find something else to occupy our time.

The Exchange Program

Rest assured, one day we will all shed this false self. We have to because one day we will all return to our true selves; our spiritual selves. Ego begins to form our identity when we are children and blossoms as we hit our teenage years. Girls strive to be pretty, well-liked, and part of the "right clique." Boys are much the same elbowing their way into the "in crowd."

Every kid in school is trying to make his or her mark in one way or another, be it as a member the football team, cheerleading squad, or debate team. For some kids, fitting in is simply a matter of survival. After graduation, however, we continue to carry this belief into our adult years, exchanging our places as football players, cheer-leaders, and debaters for a seat in the corporate world. It is the same mentality, just a different false need.

The question is: When do we shed this false self? For some, it is when we go through the experiences of life and the act of living and learning. For others, the false self will be shed when the beliefs they once held as truth no longer make sense. In many cases it will take a life-altering event or major crisis and a renewed purpose in life before we will shed our false selves.

Powerless

Do you remember the week of August 14, 2003? Half of the country and parts of Canada had a two-day blackout. The whole grid was down: no television, computers, microwaves, vacuums, blenders, or any of the other electrical "conveniences" we have come to rely on. We even had to remember what a four-way stop was, if we were brave enough to venture out to travel.

Eventually, what happened was a banding together of neighbors to get through the "crisis." People no longer believed in the separation of living in a cocoon. Because of the sweltering heat, neighbors checked on neighbors, people fired up the barbecue and cooked food that would have otherwise gone bad, and invited anyone who was within ear-shot to come and grab a bite. People even sat around and "talked."

People turned away, at least temporarily, from the part of the ego that does nothing and cares even less. They left the ego behind and turned to the spiritual side. Since the ego and spirit are not interchangeable, one had to go.

At some point in life we will all permanently shed this ego, because it is the only way to return. By returning to our natural state of being and knowing our place in the world, we gain humility, and humility is how ego is defeated.

How Far Have We Come?

The greatest revelation of our generation is the discovery that human beings,
by changing the inner attitudes of their minds,
can change the outer aspects of their lives.
—WILLIAM JAMES (1842–1910)
AMERICAN PSYCHOLOGIST AND PHILOSOPHER

I was watching a television program about time capsules. The show talked about what the purpose of a time capsule was, along with the difference between the intentional and the unintentional time capsule. Noted capsule historians are less than enthused with innocuous contents like eight-track tapes, Rubik's Cubes, and newspaper clippings. They would prefer to see significant pieces of data and technology as a better gauge as to how we lived as a society during a specific period of time.

The idea behind the time capsule is a means of communicating with people years from now by filling a capsule with photographs, documents, and other historical pieces from today. Historians have argued that the items placed inside have no historical value, offering little information as to how the initiators actually lived and how technologically advanced they were.

If you can put aside the historical argument and see the time capsule from a lighter side, it is really pretty amazing and interesting. If we were able to put our thoughts, actions, ideals, and behaviors into a time capsule, what you would discover time and time again is that nothing has really changed.

1–800 Call Cicero

It has been over two thousand years since Marcus Tullius Cicero (106–43 BC) wrote *The Six Mistakes of Man*. Cicero started out as a lawyer, became a great Roman philosopher, and eventually found his way into the political arena.

Under the autocracy that was Julius Caesar (100–44 BC), Cicero had his political hopes dashed. Caesar's murder then opened the door for Cicero's return into politics—only to be silenced forever by Mark Antony. Cicero's contributions were not from his attempted political statements, but rather his philosophical brilliance.

I have chosen *The Six Mistakes of Man* to illustrate the points that Cicero so passionately wrote about over two thousand years ago, trying to instill Greek philosophy into the decision-making process of his fellow Romans.

I will address each mistake as Cicero addressed them, and then offer examples of how each still applies in our world today. I also ask that you pay close attention to these six areas, and ask yourself how they apply to your own life.

The Six Mistakes of Man
(Cicero, Roman Writer and Philosopher, 106–43 BC)

1. **The Delusion that Personal Gain is Made by Crushing Others.**
The mistake that Cicero writes of is just as prevalent today as it was over two thousand years ago—maybe even more so. This "mistake" intertwines with motivational speeches, books, tapes, and infomercials. These programs promise us the world is fair, even though we get taken advantage of by situations and people who respond to certain market conditions. The irony here is that the only person making money is the person or persons selling the faulty idea, not the person who spends their hard-earned money on a program that typically does not work long-term.

There are certain universal laws that apply to everyone and everything; they are absolute and indisputable. The law of compensation, which is similar to cause and effect, states what we will receive in terms of material and spiritual gains and addresses events in your life. You have heard it said in different ways—"What you put out is what you get back"; "What goes around comes around"; and from the Scripture, "You reap what you sow" (Gal. 6.1–10). In other words, those who do the crushing will also receive the crushing.

Too many of us see other people as dispensable items instead of our spiritual equal. To be treated with both dignity and respect is not only what we all deserve, but it is our birthright. In lectures, I use the analogy of a roll of paper towels. You cannot treat others like a roll of paper towels, pulling them off one by one to clean up the messes of life, only to throw the paper towel away when it has no more use. Eventually the roll of paper towels will be empty, just like our lives.

The best way to get ahead in life is to put your efforts into assisting others. The way to develop long-term success is by learning cooperation and not by crushing others. You are reading the words written by someone who truly understands this. When you live from this perspective, God will place the people that you need for success in your life, at the right time and place. If your wish is to have the nicest home on the block, focus your energies on *your* home, not the destruction of the homes around you.

2. The Tendency to Worry About Things That Cannot Be Changed or Corrected. This is another mistake made when we trust our ego and push God away. Worry is something many have learned to do, yet it is a mechanism never leading to a positive outcome. *You simply cannot worry enough to make a problem go away.*

There is a radio spot for a law firm where an attorney says to the listeners, "We don't want you to worry about your problems, because that's our job." Do you really believe these attorneys are worried about your problems? Worry is a by-product of thinking through our ego, instead of thinking from our true nature.

In *A Course in Miracles* (Foundation for Inner Peace, 1975), it says, "You can learn nothing from the ego—because the ego knows nothing." So, what do we learn from this practice called worry? To address worry from a spiritually logical perspective is really very simple. If there is a challenge present in your life that you have no control over, then why worry about it?

Worry, anxiety, and all the other self-induced madness we bring on are our emotions taking over. We see it all the time—people racing around trying to get this and that finished. People worry about their health, their finances, their appearance, or their social standing. The truth is, those things we believe we should worry about ALL have solutions. *A whirlwind of activity is not the same as taking action.*

Trusting in the God who created us, unlimited in what is possible, will deliver us to a solution—*even if we believe the solution is worry.* Here is a Buddhist story about worrying that I heard during a Sunday sermon: "A man was walking down a road when suddenly he turned around to see a grizzly bear bearing down on him very quickly. In a panic, the man began to sprint as fast as he could and soon discovered he had run out of road. As he peered over the cliff, a tiger was staring up towards him. Caught between the bear and the tiger, the man decided to jump over the cliff. Sticking out of the side of the cliff was a branch the man was able to grab. On this branch were some berries, which the man decided to eat. With the bear reaching down to claw him, and the tiger jumping up trying to tear him apart, he simply decided to eat berries."

The moral of the story is, do not look back at the past or up to the future with worry—relax and just eat the berries. Stay in the moment, because the moment is all we are given; trust in the power from where you came.

THOUGHT TO PONDER—*Think about a time in your life when you worried so much about what was in front of you that worry solved the problem.*

3. Insisting That a Thing Is Impossible Because We Cannot Accomplish It. People hate what they cannot conquer. Peace seems to be one of these things; something impossible, because hatred has been one of our greatest accomplishments. We live in bodies with incredibly limitless minds. Conditioned with limitations, we cannot see the infinite when it comes to what is truly possible. What we perceive as limits has forced us to view the world through the vision of the micro rather than the macro.

We have all heard at some point in our lives what we can and cannot do. We have heard the phrases: "Understand your limitations," "Do not make waves," or "Just try to fit in." These phrases produce the mindset that has become our society, those failing to meet their true potential. If you were to go to the library, I doubt that you will find a book written by someone who played it safe and made a difference in this world.

We come from a place without limits, created by a Creator who did not perceive any limitations in His creations. Remember, through God, all things are possible. We are living in a time of incredible technological and medical advances. Just fifty years ago, people could never have imagined some of our greatest accomplishments. In the late 1980s, Tim Berners-Lee, the director of the World Wide Web Consortium (W3C), had the vision of one day linking the world together through the Internet, and in 1989 he received credit for inventing the World Wide Web.

Who would have thought that we would be able to type a message on a computer, hit the SEND key, and seconds later, the message could be received by someone halfway around the world. People with a vision do not sit around and listen to those who tell them things cannot be done. They are not necessarily individuals of supreme intelligence, or gifted in a way we are not. They simply fail to look at anything as *impossible*.

4. Refusing to Set Aside Trivial Preferences. The ego does not recognize anything as being trivial, it only recognizes being right. This is evident with many family members who no longer speak to one another. Somewhere along the way, the need to be right and prove another wrong becomes a major hurdle to accepting another's point of view. When it came to trivial nonsense, my father used to say, "Don't sweat the small stuff, and it is all small stuff."

In the big picture of life, trivial preferences are all small stuff, yet we expend so much energy trying to make them issues of greater importance. Emotions of anguish and drama take front and center over simply agreeing to disagree and letting go. Once everything is said and done, what we see as differences makes no difference at all.

I know of two sisters who had a disagreement over a trivial issue more than ten years ago. To this day, neither sister will speak to the other, even though they live only two doors apart. Holidays with family members are done in shifts; their spouses are the ones sending out the cards. Their battle is a trivial one over where one of the sisters attends church.

We are the only ones who see our trivial problems as real. We are so self-absorbed in what bothers us, we fail to see a host of other things that should capture our attention—things like worldwide oppression, poverty, starvation, and natural disasters.

We, on the other hand, complain because there is not enough selection at the all-you-can-eat buffet; Get steamed when we have to wait more than thirty seconds to purchase a five-dollar latté; Feel it is necessary to badger wait staff because they are not attentive to our every need; Or wonder how we are going to be able to get through the day when we have only three hundred and fifty cable channels to choose from.

We will never all think alike, act alike, or live by the same codes, and that is perfectly fine. It is not our job to point out what we do and do not like when it comes to the preferences of other people. Get into the practice of acting and responding from your spiritual self, your real true self, which teaches kindness and compassion, and remember, "Don't sweat the small stuff!"

5. Neglecting Development and Refinement of the Mind, and Not Acquiring the Habit of Reading and Studying. Considering the fact that the number one health issue in both children and adults is obesity, do you think it is possible that Cicero saw the dawning of the Xbox®, Playstation®, and text messaging, as the best way for us to occupy our spare time?

It is my contention that if you were to ask a child what was the last thing he or she did, read a book, or play a video game, the answer would be obvious. Books sit on the shelves gathering dust, while joysticks and keyboards garner the attention of the youngster. In our society, more often than not, families have both parents in the workforce, and the tendency is to allow children more leisure time.

I heard on the radio that obesity in children actually increases during the summer months—why in the summer months? The answer is simple. Not being in school means more time for uninspiring activities, a part of *The Six Mistakes of Man* that Cicero offered us over two thousand years ago.

Physical activity plays an important role in keeping our bodies operating at an optimum level. When we do not take the time everyday to give the body what it needs, it responds back in the appearance of excess weight, lack of motivation, loss of interests, and over time, internal breakdowns. In other words, the body responds back with what is given, and the mind is no different.

Mental gymnastics are equally as necessary. Acquiring knowledge, reading a variety of topics, and the lost art of study keep the mind sharp and in a cognitive flow. Reading and studying do not end when you receive your degree or diploma. We are enrolled in the school of life-long learning, and graduation day is not one which you will celebrate and forget about what was learned.

It is true that we are all teachers, but we are also students who need to learn as well as teach. Magazines, periodicals, and the Internet, provide us with rich learning experiences about other people, cultures, sciences, and technology. Cable television is another source of good programming, giving us insight into many of these areas as well, but we tend to gravitate to the lowest form of energy sources out there: Jerry Springer, the local news, mindless reality shows, and so on. Take the time to spend at least one hour per day learning something new, or adding to what you already know on a subject.

Engage the mind; feed it what it needs to run at an optimum level. The things you may learn will certainly affect the way you think, feel, and believe. Someone once said, "The greatest study we can receive is the study that gives us no grade, no advancement, or a new title. The greatest study is what we do because we want to do it and learn from it."

6. Attempting to Compel Others to Believe and Live As We do. I ask you, is there no greater mistake that Cicero wrote about than this one? By definition, to compel is to "force somebody to do something." Compelling another person completely removes all principles from the anthem of God's free will; compelling can only be accomplished through fear, threat, control, and manipulation, which are all very low source states of energy.

People who truly live by spiritual truth are unable to compel anyone into doing anything. A spiritual soul loves and respects; it never forces. We all know what is best for us; however, when you go as far as telling someone else what is best for them, this is a disturbing thought. I certainly cannot speak to what prompted Cicero to write about this mistake; however, in our day and time I will offer this observation. Compelling others has become a part of everyday life. You can find it in politics, religion, unions, Hollywood, and professional sports.

I see organized religion as one of the biggest offenders of this mistake; the examples are many and the results are tragic. In my opinion, religion has missed so much when it comes to the "message." Many religions often interpret the written word in a completely different way than it was originally intended. Some religious zealots, such as Hitler and the Ayatollah Khomeini, end up becoming the most dangerous people on the planet when they compel others to adhere to their beliefs. Not only do they tell each other how to live, but they feel compelled to tell you and I how to live as well.

Compelling others to think and believe as we do is a strategy that will not float in the minds of people who live their lives based on a set of principles and values that make sense only to them. One size does not fit all. This mistake can only create greater hatred and resentment. To believe *one way is the only way* is just plain ridiculous. Patience, understanding, tolerance, and compassion must be our stronghold if we ever hope to live as instructed by our Creator.

Two Thousand Years Worth of Philosophy

Well there you have it, *The Six Mistakes of Man*, written over two thousand years ago by a philosopher attempting to bring morality to the Romans using Greek philosophy.

As we have recently come into the twenty-first century, we find that many things have changed for the better, yet some things have not changed since the beginning of time; such things as ego consciousness, fear, power, and control.

What we should have learned by now is that these actions do not bear good and bountiful fruit. When you talk about decency, conduct, and manners, our lives are not about learning but rather about returning back to our natural form. This natural form is our spiritual self, which is the part of us that understands that learning is returning.

Universal Disease

Collective fear stimulates herd instinct, and tends to produce ferocity toward those who are not regarded as members of the herd.
—BERTRAND RUSSELL (1872–1970)
BRITISH PHILOSOPHER

It has been seventeen years since my aunt lost a long, tough battle with cancer. During those last few years the insidious disease slowly occupied her body and we were forced to watch this once elegant woman waste away. The final days ticked off slowly as she was kept alive by tubes administering a variety of pain medications.

My aunt took on the cancer as she did everything else in her turbulent life—with unshakable faith and courage. Her cancer was one of many challenges she faced in a life confronted with obstacles. The one thing about this disease is that it comes and finds you; recklessly destroying your body with swiftness and vigor.

Cancer is a goal-oriented disease, and the primary goal is to destroy every healthy cell in your body. Cancer is also non-discriminatory in deciding on its victims. It does not care how much money you have, how young you may be, or what kind of person you are.

Geographically it is willing to travel to all points of the globe, and once it invades it can be very difficult to chase away.

Hatred is also a disease with a single mission—it seeks to destroy. Hatred is defined as a feeling of immense dislike toward another person, group, or thing. These feelings may cause a person to want to kill, harm, or avoid that person or thing. Unlike cancer, which seeks you out, you must seek out hatred, and invite it to come live within your heart.

Are We Born to Hate?

There was a case on Court TV where the accused was on trial for committing a hate crime. On the witness stand for the defense was an expert in the field of behavioral science. On direct examination of the witness, the defense attorney questioned the possibility of hatred being hard-wired into each of us at birth.

If you are like me, you will have a difficult time swallowing this idea for one main reason: Children come into this world with zero preconceived notions or judgments toward anyone or anything—all they know is love. Newborns do not enter this world with a swastika on their forehead, nor has a parent ever told me that their child's first words were, "I hate you." Hatred is a learned behavior and the idea it is pre-wired is absurd.

I think the main job for every parent is simply to keep their kids safe because children have no understanding or experience with fear. The first learning lessons come from those we are closest to: Mom and Dad, aunts and uncles, grandmas and grandpas, etc.

As a writer, I don't enjoy writing about this subject. As a reader, you probably don't enjoy reading about it. The subject, however, must be talked about openly if we ever hope to see any lasting change—no matter how uncomfortable we may feel.

It's Only a Verb

I am sure that you use the word "hate" in everyday life—I have as well. We use it to describe how a shirt looks on us, how certain foods taste, or to describe TV shows we watch. When the word is used to describe how one feels toward a specific group of people, well, that is something completely different. Anytime we use a broad brush to identify a group as a whole, we are expressing ignorance and bigotry.

John Amaechi, a former professional basketball player, wrote a book called *Man in the Middle*, published by ESPN Books, in which he revealed that he was gay. Around the same time on a Miami, Florida, radio station another professional basketball player, Tim Hardaway, was asked by the host his opinion about playing basketball with a gay teammate. Hardaway's response was to say: "First of all, I wouldn't want him on my team; Second of all, if he was on my team, I would really distance myself from him because I don't think that it's right and I don't think he should be in the locker room when we're in the locker room."[1]

---

[1] Mark Woods, Coming out fighting off basketball court, *Scotland on Sunday*, interview February 18, 2007.

Following Hardaway's response the host said to him, "You know what you are saying there is flatly homophobic. It's bigotry." To which Hardaway responded, "Well *you* know I hate gay people, so I let it be known. I don't like gay people and I don't like to be around gay people. I am homophobic, I don't like it. It shouldn't be in the world or in the United States, so yeah, I don't like it."

Mr. Hardaway quickly apologized for his comments in a radio interview with Fox affiliate WSVN in Miami. He stated, "Yes, I regret it. I'm sorry. I shouldn't have said I hate gay people or anything like that. That was my mistake." He also later added that "being an African-American, I should have shown more sensitivity." An apology is the correct path to take as long as the words are sincere.

In the Eyes of God

The question that is usually asked of me is "How can you condone such a lifestyle?" I think because of ego, we have over-emphasized what our position is in life. We have stepped out of the assigned position of serving others to assuming the position of judging others. I see each and every person as an equal, as a child of God, no better or different than I am and without prejudice.

We are all created the same, in that we want certain God-given rights be extended to us, as well as extending those gifts to other people without qualification. Everybody deserves to be treated with dignity and respect, regardless how we feel about them. This type of approach allows me to live my life as it was intended to be experienced; leaving the value of judging others to those who believe it is up to them to categorize each and every person they come into contact with.

God made our assignments here on earth pretty simple to understand: Be kind to one another, feed one another, serve one another, and love each other as I have loved you. Seems to me those are easy to follow, very specific instructions. Somewhere along the line, many of us decided that incorporating hatred into our lives was the proper way to live. It's not. Ask yourself if there has ever been a situation where you hated something so much, that the hatred in your heart ended up making you feel better?

Not Our Finest Moment

So what are the answers to combat against the very thing threatening our existence? I wish I knew. I wish I could understand and explain why two men in Wyoming beat a man and then hung him on a fence because he was gay. I wish I could figure out why three men in Texas chained a black man to the bumper of their truck, dragging him until his body disintegrated.

Sometimes during the evening news you will hear a leader of some country shout out a familiar theme regarding one of their neighbors. "We hate these people because. . . ." "We hate that country because. . . ." "We don't acknowledge that countries right to exist because. . . ." "If it wasn't for those people the world would be a better place because. . . ."

There are conflicts happening all over the world—civil wars, wars of oppression, wars that were started thousands of years ago, and wars just because. We are told the leaders of those countries feel justified in weeding out and killing as many people as possible, and that the innocent lives taken are simply collateral damage in unavoidable conflicts. The usual defense is, "God is on our side."

Once in a While We Get It Right

My father told me the following story that took place during World War II between German and American soldiers. Three American soldiers looking for shelter came upon an isolated cottage in the Ardennes Forest near the German-Belgium border. Fritz Vincken, who was twelve-years-old at the time, and his mother Elisabeth, took refuge in the cabin that had been in the family after their original home had been destroyed.

On this bitter cold Christmas Eve in 1944, the American soldiers, carrying one of their wounded, asked Elisabeth Vincken for food and shelter. She agreed to let them in knowing that aiding the enemy could cost her life, but only after the soldiers agreed to leave their weapons outside.

Soon there was another knock at the door, which sent Fritz and his mother into a panic. They knew that these were the Germans coming for the Americans. Quick thinking on Elisabeth's part saved her life as she told the Germans that they too could come into her home for shelter and a hot meal only if they also agreed to keep their weapons outside. Oddly enough, the soldiers complied with her request.

Try to imagine what that original face-to-face encounter between the Americans and Germans must have been like. How was it possible that anything good could have come from a situation like this? After all, this was World War II and the Germans and Americans were sworn enemies.

Elisabeth Vincken read from the Bible and declared that since it was Christmas Eve, she wanted no one, not even the Germans or Americans, to fight on this peaceful holy night. The soldiers sat there sharing a hot meal and one of the German soldiers, a medical student, helped the wounded American soldier. The men began to see themselves as human beings and not enemies—each as a child of the Creator.

After a peaceful night's sleep, the Germans and Americans said their goodbyes and went their separate ways. The Germans even gave the Americans a compass so they could find their way back. This event took place because of a remarkable woman who truly understood the meaning of "peace on earth."

Can Six Become 6 Million?

If six men who were sworn to hate and kill each other can come away with a new awareness simply by sitting and talking, coming together on a level of friendship, kindness, and understanding, why can't we do the same only on a much larger stage? These six men developed a new awareness, simply remembering something we all know, but fail to practice in our everyday lives—*If You Only Knew What You Already Know.*

We must ultimately get back to this place or our existence, as we know it, will no longer continue. Hatred will be what kills us all. We can only blame ourselves, not God, not some dark force—just us.

Practicing patience, understanding, and forgiveness is the only way, but the ego will never surrender to this thought. Patience, understanding, and forgiveness are not signs of weakness but signs of strength. Mark Twain once described the act of forgiving this way, "Forgiveness is the fragrance that the violet sheds to the heel that crushed it."

Hatred on the Home Front

On April 19, 1995, this country experienced the greatest act of domestic terrorism perpetrated on American soil. On that day a little after 9 a.m., parents had just finished dropping off their kids at day care in the Alfred P. Murrah Federal Building in downtown Oklahoma City. A few minutes later a rental truck parked in front of the building exploded taking out half of the building. A nation sat mesmerized for the next two weeks as the bodies of 168 men, women, and children were pulled from the rubble. The image of firefighter Chris Fields holding a dying infant also was burned into our collective minds.

It did not take the authorities very long to find a suspect. Just an hour and a half after the explosion, Gulf War veteran Timothy McVeigh was pulled over for driving without a license plate as he fled the scene. Fortunately, just before he was about to be released, he was recognized and eventually charged.

Following a highly publicized trial, McVeigh was found guilty and received the death penalty. He waived all of his rights of appeal and was given an execution date of May 16th, 2001. In a letter to Fox News, McVeigh tried to make sense of what he did. "I chose to bomb a federal building because such action served more purposes than other options. Foremost, the bombing was a retaliatory strike; a counter attack, for the cumulative raids that federal agents had participated in over the preceding years...."[2]

As the execution date loomed, the federal government failed to turn over requested papers to the defense. This oversight resulted in postponing the date for execution, which enraged the public. You would hear comments by members of the media calling this a ploy by his attorneys just to delay the execution date, but eventually the date was rescheduled for June 11, 2001. The crowd began arriving early at the federal prison in Terre Haute, Indiana. Some carried signs, some held candles, and some were just there out of morbid curiosity.

At 7:17 a.m., the Warden stepped to the microphone and announced that Timothy McVeigh had been pronounced dead. I can only assume that at 7:18 a.m., everyone thirsting for this moment took the back of their hand, wiped their forehead, and thought, "Damn, do I feel better." We hear this word "closure" thrown around like a football in mini-camp. The death of another person is no cause for fist pumping and certainly has no soul-cleansing properties.

A New Perspective

Bud Welch had a very unique perspective on the Oklahoma City bombing. He was waiting for a call from his daughter, Julie Marie, that morning. Julie was an interpreter for the Social Security Administration

---

[2] McVeigh's letter to Fox News, Thursday, April 26, 2001.

and worked out of the Alfred P. Murrah Federal Building. It was normal for the two of them to get together for lunch at a local restaurant across from where she worked. Her call never came. Instead, Bud received a call from his brother-in-law and was told to turn on the television. After watching the coverage of the blast, he waited two days by the phone for a call that never came.

Julie Marie Welch was only eighteen feet away from the bomb when it went off. She was found the following morning and was one of the 168 people killed that day. Julie Marie graduated from Marquette University and spoke five languages. She was also a devoted Catholic and loving daughter. Her plan was to marry a lieutenant she had met from the Tinker Air Force Base.

Bud Welch wasn't interested in a long, drawn-out trial. In his words, "I was opposed to the death penalty all my life until my daughter Julie Marie was killed in the Oklahoma City bombing. For many months after the bombing I could have killed Timothy McVeigh myself. Temporary insanity is real, and I have lived it. You can't think of enough adjectives to describe the rage, revenge, and hate, I felt. But after time, I was able to examine my conscience, and I realized that if McVeigh is put to death, it won't help me in the healing process. People talk about executions bringing closure. But how can there be closure when my little girl is never coming back. I finally realized that the death penalty is all about revenge and hate, and revenge and hate are why Julie Marie and 167 others are dead."[3]

---

[3] Don't Kill in Our Names: Families of Murder Victims Speak Out Against the Death Penalty (Rutgers University Press, February 14, 2003).

He began to give up his hatred to something he did not understand. I was able to interview him and asked the following question: "Many spiritual advances occur in the face of horrific events. Was this true in your case?" He told me he did not know what took place, something just happened. He realized that he was not the only victim in this tragedy. The McVeigh family was suffering as well. "Timothy's father's pain had to be incredible," said Bud. "As best I can tell, he did everything right."

As the execution date drew near, the media repeatedly asked Bud if he was glad this day had finally arrived. Bud reiterated, "Revenge is nothing but hate and anger. We have to stop the carnage, stop ratcheting up the violence, and stop all the killing. Execution is no solution." No matter how many times he was asked, his answer never swayed. "I have forgiven Mr. McVeigh; he killed out of revenge and hatred; to kill him is revenge and hatred."

Spirit vs. Ego

Six months after the bombing, a poll was taken of families and survivors. They were asked if they were still in favor of the execution and 85% said yes. Another poll was taken six years after the execution and that number fell to half. Today many say it was a mistake. You don't die from a snake bite; it is the venom that spreads inside of you that eventually kills you. Revenge and hatred work the same way, it is not the devastation of the act that kills, it is letting it work its way inside that does the devastation.

Forgiveness frees us from the bonds of hatred and is the most powerful thing you can do for your spirit. It frees us from ego which wants to be at war, creating chaos, unrest, and turmoil. Take a look around. Are there people in your life who are incapable of forgiveness? They are easily recognizable. They are quickly angered, have trouble relaxing, and are very cynical.

Those who cannot forgive people around them live through ego—the false self. Spirituality does not recognize the bonds of hatred because hatred is an attitude that keeps us in darkness. Do not listen to your ego. Do not fall prey to hatred. Listen only to God because God and Spirit are one, and God does not deceive.

The Wolves Within

An old grandfather said to his grandson, who came to him with anger at a friend who had done him an injustice, "Let me tell you a story. I, too, at times, have felt a great hate for those that have taken so much, with no sorrow for what they do."

"But hate wears you down, and does not hurt your enemy. It is like taking poison and wishing your enemy would die. I have struggled with these feelings many times."

He continued, "It is as if there are two wolves inside me. One is good and does no harm. He lives in harmony with all around him, and does not take offense when no offense was intended. He will only fight when it is right to do so, and in the right way."

"But the other wolf, ah! He is full of anger. The littlest thing will set him into a fit of temper. He fights everyone, all the time, for no reason. He cannot think because his anger and hate are so great. It is helpless anger, for his anger will change nothing."

"Sometimes, it is hard to live with these two wolves inside me, for both of them try to dominate my spirit."

The boy looked intently into his Grandfather's eyes and asked, "Which one wins, Grandfather?"

The Grandfather smiled and quietly said, "The one I feed."

Ask yourself this question: Which of the wolves are you feeding?

~

Calling Off the Search

People spend a lifetime searching for happiness, looking for peace.
They chase idle dreams, addictions, religions, even other people,
hoping to fill the emptiness that plagues them.
The irony is that the only place they ever needed to search was within.
—RAMONA L. ANDERSEN (1887–1949)
AMERICAN WRITER

It is something available to all who desire it; it comes in different sizes, varying amounts, and is very inexpensive. It has no fats, carbs, or bad cholesterol. It will have a marvelous effect on your body and nervous system, and it lowers your blood pressure. It will not break down because of high mileage and the warranty never expires. It is abundant, regardless of the situation. It requires no special education, unique talent, or gift. It is always in fashion, God-given, and all you have to do is nurture it.

For many, this thing I write about is elusive, found only through pursuit, and rarely attained—this thing is called *happiness*. In order to fully understand and experience true happiness, we must understand that happiness is an internal state. I will frequently refer to internal states, because we often forget, for various reasons, that nothing is really accomplished through our external self. The same is true for happiness.

The Chase Is On

When we believe things are missing in our lives, we usually take the action of pursuit. When we chase after something, it is because we feel we do not have enough of it. This is classic ego logic. You cannot find happiness in your pockets, in the cushions of the couch, or most dangerously, in another person. The only place you can find it is in yourself.

I grew up on the east side of Detroit, Michigan; our house was Kid Central because we had a swimming pool. The pool was nothing special. It stood about three feet high with a flimsy metal wall, but we used that pool every day throughout the summer. Our primary job was to just keep water in it. As the summer went on, so did the need to replenish the water in the pool. Over time, the liner started to crack and tear from the hot summer sun and the abuse from the occupants.

We tried to repair the liner using measures only children could concoct. We tried to staple it back together, duct tape it, used super glue, and even put bricks over the wounds. The tears in the liner, however, continued to grow, eventually giving way to large rips. The liner could no longer hold water and ultimately the pool died a natural death.

The Perfect Storm

I tell this story because it illustrates a connection to the human experience. You cannot fill your heart and soul with happiness if you have rips and tears internally. It simply will not work. The rips and tears of the soul represent lethal levels of low source energy which I refer to as traumatic events, poor decision-making, and the emotion attached to each one of these states. When we allow this energy to fester, grow, or even worse, pretend it does not exist, this energy consumes our every thought, action, and decision-making process.

Ego consciousness coupled with internal imbalance is the perfect storm, because western philosophy is very external in what we have been led to believe happiness represents. This type of consciousness was introduced, stamped, and sanctioned. We have been sold a bill of goods through every media outlet. The answer to your perceived unhappiness can be solved through many different external methods. We know this is totally false. The real work is internal and for many this prescription can be messy. Why choose something that is difficult to deal with, when there are much easier options on the table?

Opposite Ends of the Spectrum

I heard a radio spot recently that addressed the external approach to happiness and the false promise that comes with the proclamation. The promotion was from a doctor who specialized in breast alterations. His catch phrase was, "If you want to feel better, then fill out that sweater." These professionals almost appear as predators, lying in wait for easily succumbing targets.

Television is another popular outlet for delivering the message of promise. You see countless advertisements promoting drugs, diets, and exercise equipment—anything to move someone to take action. People will go anywhere or do anything to get answers, but in the long run those answers fail all expectations. Why? Because the source of their obesity and poor health are inside, not outside.

Does the name Chris Farley sound familiar? Chris is thought of by many as one of the greatest successes on the long-running, late-night comedy show, *Saturday Night Live* (SNL). David Spade, a friend and actor, once referred to him as "the funniest man in America." Chris had it all at one point. He had adoring fans everywhere and enjoyed financial success. Chris was able to manage everything in his life, except his internal self. His life ended tragically and abruptly on the floor of a Chicago apartment from an overdose of drugs and alcohol. Internally, Chris Farley was bankrupt.

I offer an alternate example—Nelson Mandela. Mandela was an outspoken lawyer who talked openly about the injustices in his country, South Africa. Mandela spent twenty years in prison—solitary confinement no less, but left prison with forgiveness in his heart. Internally, there was nothing that could have been done to him that could shake him of his beliefs.

The changes you make externally will not change who you are. You can display shadows of external happiness, but internal obesity will expose who you are, giving people little choice in how they react to you.

In Love with Fear

People experience many different emotions. However, there are only two that govern who we are—love and fear. All that you experience comes from one of these two. Ideally, we are driven towards love and away from fear. An internal diet will shed those emotional pounds and keep them off permanently. Unlike external weight, internal weight is causing a much greater problem by imposing life-threatening consequences.

Just as we all desire to have external success, we must have internal success as well, to give us a feeling of balance. The two work together to provide a sense of peace and harmony. You no doubt heard the expression "You cannot be in two places at the same time." We do not experience states of low source energy and high source energy simultaneously. The best cosmetic work you can do for yourself is the work you do for your soul. This is where true transformation begins and life-changing results occur.

Life is results. Behaviors are directors. Repeat the same behavior, get the same result. The definition of insanity is to repeat the same behavior and expect a different result. You can alter your internal reality with drugs, alcohol, gambling, sex, or whichever poison you choose. But at the end of the day, you are still the same person with the same issues.

Internal imbalance is like a hurricane and the eye of the storm is your soul. Internal weight is a taxing burden that will destroy the heart, soul, and mind. When our internal self is out of alignment, the part of us that sees life the way it was intended to be experienced

71

is blinded. Feelings that invoke those of high energy states cannot come to a troubled mind. Internal obesity causes us to be cynical and suspicious. If you have no love in your heart, how can you give it to other people?

Reality TV in an Unreal World

One day while flipping through cable stations, I caught a syndicated television show. The guests were two women who I assumed were recovering from severe burns. As I continued to watch, I learned these women were not recovering from burns at all—they were talking about their experiences with plastic surgery. *As a frightening side note, in Beverly Hills, California, there are over four thousand plastic surgeons and only four hundred pediatricians!*

The first woman spoke to the audience about her procedures. She was twenty-eight and had twenty-six procedures done to date. The second woman, who had had every type of liposuction procedure available, was preparing for another. Her husband, now working three jobs to cover their bulging debt, told her the next one would be the last or he was going leave. By the way, the first woman went back for another nose procedure. Now she needed Q-tips to keep her air passages open so she could breathe. Her surgeon told her in no uncertain terms, "One more procedure and your face will cave in." Her response was simply to state, "I am willing to roll the dice."

For the life of me, I will never understand how these professionals, in good conscience, continue to destroy these people. They must be able to recognize a problem when it is staring them right in the face. There should be some responsibility. You cannot fix an automobile that is not running by simply washing and applying a coat of wax. We must first engage the problem from under the hood to appreciate the external beauty.

A Medicated Society Is a Polite Society

Today, more than ever, society is under a constant assault from the pharmaceutical companies who offer solutions to the perpetually unhappy—it's the basic theory of "open wide" and swallow a pill and happiness will be here soon. In his stand up routine (**I'm Telling You for the Last Time**), Jerry Seinfeld described the way pharmaceutical companies see us—"no face, mouth open."

I try not to watch a lot of television. The times I do, however, it is almost a certainty that a commercial for the latest medication to hit the market will saturate the airwaves. Usually the spot begins with the afflicted person describing what his or her life was like until they decided to visit a doctor. Then, a scene change and you see people frolicking through a flowery meadow, playing football with children, enjoying potato salad at a picnic—always on a sun-drenched afternoon. Then you hear the words "this medication is not for everyone." The narrator tells of the possible side effects of taking the described medication. The narrator continues. "You should not take this pill if you are nursing or have liver problems. Do not operate heavy machinery. You may experience sweating, tremors, nausea, dizziness, or an uncontrollable desire to chase cars."

We Are Cured

In 1987 we were introduced to a pill that came with a promise of elevating the mood of the clinically depressed—the promise of Prozac. Prozac very quickly became the drug of choice for sufferers of depression. Today, this pill is swallowed by millions of people, including more and more children that are somehow diagnosed as clinically depressed. Veterinarians have even been known to give a script for Fido when he is off his game a little.

These classes of antidepressants are responsible for slowing down how the brain absorbs serotonin. This neurotransmitter will constrict blood vessels at points where injuries occur, and may affect emotional states. By successfully altering brain chemistry, we can elevate our mood as well.

Serotonin is found in the brain and tissue of everyone, not only the clinically depressed. If taking this antidepressant will make you feel better, or it is prescribed to do this, why not take this drug if you are not a depressed person? Why not allow every Tom, Dick, and Harriet to swallow these magic pills?

Obviously it is because of the risks that come with this type of medication. Some risks including insomnia, nausea, and loss of appetite are considered mild. Other risks are more extreme and include agitation, anxiety, increased hostility, violent outbursts, and suicidal thoughts. We have even seen examples of people committing unspeakable crimes while on SSRI's (Selective Serotonin Reuptake Inhibitors). Examples include: Columbine, Red Lake Indian Reservation, the Amish school shooting, Virginia Tech, and most recently the Nebraska Mall rampage.

A Time in My Life

I believe there is a huge difference between being sad and being depressed. When I was growing up, I would become upset and sad when I would not get picked to play basketball, when I would get beat up at school, or when I would get teased or bullied. It is called the childhood experience and we all have had to deal with it. Is it possible these medications interfere with the natural development of children?

There was a time in my own life when I was convinced something was wrong with me, so I visited a doctor. The doctor and I talked maybe forty-five minutes when the diagnosis came back to me that I had a condition known as bipolar. I was immediately medicated and told by the doctor that help was on the way. I stuck with the program for ninety days and felt the same as I did the day I started, which I expected would be the case.

Understand that this is not an indictment of medication, psychology, or to impugn individuals who truly are in need of these classes of medications. I have witnessed some radical changes in people when they receive proper treatment. In my case, and I suspect many more, medication was not a plausible solution. For me, the changes I had to make were internal. My behavior and treatment of other people, taking advantage of and cheating on them, was a condition that required an internal rewiring.

When you understand how your actions affect people in a negative way, it is enough to depress anyone. You cannot swallow enough pills to elevate your consciousness to that of a spiritual existence. You must do the work, and it starts by changing the way you see yourself.

Striving but Never Arriving

The pursuit of happiness is the archetype of how we see the happiness that we believe is missing in our lives. The questions we ask ourselves usually begin with "if" or "when." *When* I get that raise at work, *when* I put my last child through college, *if* the people I care about would take a greater interest in what I am doing, then I would be happy. Yes, but for how long?

Internally, we all have a level of happiness that we return to following any event. When you drive that shiny, brand new, convertible off the showroom lot, your level of elation rises for a period of time. The same holds true in the event of a new relationship. It is the ego that has us convinced that in order to be happy, we must have something tangible that we can see or show off to other people.

The truth of what it means to be really happy is intangible. What we strive for is already located in our hearts. People that truly understand this are the happiest people of all, because there is no chase involved—no pursuit of happiness. Happiness is already found.

The "less is more, more is less approach" tells us that when you encounter individuals who are truly happy in life, they have an approach that others do not. They are not consumed with the chase, because chasing is an illusion that we created.

Keeping It in Vegas

The last time I was in Las Vegas, I was in an area where televisions were on the walls, showing sporting events from all over the world.

One of the televisions was broadcasting dog racing from Florida. The dogs were walking around calmly until herded into gates. A bell sounded, the gates opened, and the dogs chased this rabbit hanging from a horizontal pole. I can only surmise that this is how the dogs are trained to race; chasing the object in front of them becomes a learned behavior. Conditioning these animals to chase this rabbit is an illusion created through constant repetition, to the point that they just don't know any better.

We have been conditioned much the same. We constantly strive for something we can never attain through a method we have been conditioned to accept. When we are congruent with God, the chase ends. There is no reason to continue this insane practice. People who live from this perspective allow what they desire to flow to them. They trust that the way to attract happiness into life is to attract simply by being.

Universal Language

The only thing I know about love is that love is all there is....
Love can do all but raise the dead.
—EMILY DICKINSON
AMERICAN POET (1830–86)

Is there a word in our lexicon more misunderstood, more abused than the word *love*? We use the word to describe how we feel about people, pets, and a favorite color, as well as the food we eat. Love can be used to manipulate others and as a trampoline in our own emotional playground. People need to feel loved, as much as they need air to sustain life; because without love, life would be impossible.

There are really two ways to define the meaning of the word. First is the spiritual version, where guidance comes directly from God. The second is ego-based and guided by manipulation, false promises and half-truths.

We all come from a God of perfect love, a small piece of the whole, meaning if we are what we come from, then we are also perfect love. Much like happiness, love is something we desire in our lives. But there are many people whose quest for love leaves them empty and unfulfilled. It is the way they have gone about the pursuit of this missing need that is ultimately to blame.

Over the Edge

I had planned a trip to Niagara Falls in Ontario a while back—I had never been to the Falls, but it was one of the things on my bucket list. After spending the better part of the evening driving, I decided to spend the night in St. Catharines, which is in the heart of Niagara. Following registration, I was given a room key and a property map to guide me to my room.

When I reached the door, I set my bag on the floor, unlocked the door, and then began searching with my hand for the light switch. After a minute or so of fumbling around, I saw a large light attached to a retaining wall through the patio door. I opened the door leading to the patio and walked over to the wall, and as I did a short time earlier, started looking for the light switch. As I walked along the wall, I was approached by a fellow lodger asking what I was doing, and if he could help me out. I told him yes, thank you. "So what are we looking for?" he asked. I explained as I entered my room I was unable to locate the switch, saw the light outside, and decided to look out here for it. With a perplexed look on his face, he said to me, "Sir, the only place to find what you are looking for is in there, not out here."

The moral of this story is one in a lesson of truth—one you have certainly read about in this book. There is nothing in this external world that can deliver what you desire most—it must come from the internal self. We can walk the external wall all we want, but the answer is a place very close to us, a place too many do not trust. The problem is that not many people grasp this universal principal; they instead follow the heart of the false self, which means pursuing something they already have.

My Friend Betty

I have a nine-year-old boxer named Betty, and every once in a while, especially when she has an audience, she will run in circles pursuing her tail. It's funny to see, but everyone watching knows she will never get what she is chasing; the pursuer is the only one who does not understand this.

Today we have the Internet, and pursuing love has taken on a whole new meaning. Now you can pay to have someone else do the chasing for you. There are web sites that promise to find you love by simply answering a few questions. A profile is generated based on your answers which matches you with the person of your dreams. If for whatever reason this service is not able to find you a match with that "perfect someone," they will *let you know.*

How about that for a kick in the head—it is entirely possible that you are so pathetic, not even a computer can find love for you! I listened as one woman described her experience with one of these sites. She said after two failed marriages she had finally found her "soul mate" and was very thankful to the service for helping in the search. Soul mate—are you kidding? I don't believe that divorcing a couple of times and filling out a questionnaire on the Internet is a prerequisite to finding a soul mate. Something tells me that was not what God had in mind when it comes to marriage.

Profiling the Profiler

I took the time to read some of the profiles on one of these sites, and there was a common recurring theme. It seemed people liked to list all of the things that they did not want in a mate. Things like, "I don't want a person who plays the field"; "I don't want someone who is married"; "I am not looking for someone who drinks, smokes, or is unemployed." It is not with the slightest bit of irony that it seems anytime you ask for what it is you don't want, it is exactly what you end up with.

So what happens when we believe we have found that special someone? There are usually a couple of scenarios that take place at this point early in the relationship. One is the Hollywood version, like in the movie *Jerry McGuire*, when he said "You complete me." A cute Hollywood line because in the movies, love usually wins. But in the real world this application never applies. The belief that another person can complete who we are in our lives is a fallacy.

In order to be complete human beings, we have to be at peace with our internal self, comfortable in who we are and what we bring to the table. There is nothing that exists in the physical world, including another person that can fulfill us as a person; you cannot expect another to fill the inner voids that may exist within you. When we depend on someone else to "fix" what is wrong with us, the end result is usually one person losing their identity, and the other person getting exactly what they expected—the worst.

The Gift

What I am trying to say is, if you do not bring a spiritual maturity to a loving relationship, the relationship is probably going to fail. The love one has freely promised to you now becomes a proving ground for the other person to complete. The real issue is never addressed; the issue being that love and fear cannot exist simultaneously in the heart, because they are incompatible.

It is as simple as not being able to be in two places at once. True love must be pure if it is going to work. Make sure before professing your love to another that you first love yourself. If not, what you are seeking is approval and not love.

When internal unrest occupies your soul, no amount of love from another person will ever suffice; it will never be enough. In the absence of self-love you will never experience the magic of true love. As the song goes, "learning to love yourself is the greatest love of all," because without love, you will never be able to give this gift away.

Romance or Romantic Love

If we keep our thoughts focused upon a good, healthy relationship then we are *experiencing* love. If we become focused on an unhealthy relationship, then we are *using* love. Whichever path you choose, healthy or unhealthy, is what your reality will become. It is also important to remember that people who do not have love for themselves feel that no one has love for them. And you simply cannot give away what you do not have.

When we live with doubts, unresolved issues or past pains, these troubling experiences can only give way to insecurities, possessiveness and control. When we are internally incomplete, we will destroy what we claim to want more than anything. Another way we misinterpret love is through the eyes of romance or romantic love.

Have you ever watched a hockey game during the playoffs? When the puck is dropped the teams begin play at a furious, desperate pace. Each team hits a little harder, grinds a little longer, and skates a little faster, all in an effort to be the team to score first. This pace is impossible to maintain for a full sixty-minute game. Eventually the pace will slow and become predictable, which is very similar to what romantic love is. Like the magician shouting *abracadabra*, we follow the illusion until the end, only to discover that we have been fooled by the act.

Romantic love is all about a series of firsts—the first communication, first date, first embrace, first kiss, and first intimate experience. And the one that should cause you to take a few steps back—the all-important "love at first sight." All of these "firsts" cause powerful emotional surges to go through our hearts, minds, and nervous system. Until, of course, the next series of firsts—the first disagreement, first argument, or first time you see the person in a different light.

Teeter Totter of Life

I have a friend who fashions himself a professional dater—always pursuing, never arriving. When he meets a woman, he calls to tell me, usually with the same opening line. "Hey Paul, I know I have said this before, but this time I am as serious as a heart attack. I finally met Cinderella." By Thursday, Cinderella has turned into Lizzie Borden, and her flaws cover every facet of her being from the makeup she wears to the number of rings she lets the phone go before answering.

Physics tells us what goes up must come down—it is one of the universal laws. That emotionally charged adrenalin rush we experience will come down as well, and when it does you will find a human being with good points and bad. Desire, fascination, and enthusiasm fuel romantic love, and this cocktail of emotions will cause you to do things that are not normal to your routine.

What happens when the dust settles? The next logical step for two people in love is to get engaged and make plans to marry—I know a few couples currently in that situation. When I talk to them about this all important decision, I come away with the distinct impression that the marriage is being used as a way to reignite the passion they had when they began dating.

Another View

In the Hindu culture, marriage between two people is decidedly far different than marriage here in the West. Hindus traditionally pair couples by compatibility, retracing behaviors and lifestyle going back two generations. The Hindu practice certainly does not recognize love as a reason to marry; rather, how well two people are matched genetically, along with temperament and family background.

In the Hindu culture when you marry, you marry for life. Marriage is viewed as a sacrament and not a contract. It is a life-long commitment of one wife and one husband and a means of spiritual growth. Marriage for Hindus is considered a union between two families rather then between two young people. The husband and wife see each other each with all their strengths and weaknesses. Divorce is not usually an option. Hindu civil code only permits divorce on certain grounds, but the religion as such does not approve of divorce and as such is very rare. In the West, marriages get flushed away like draft beer at a frat party, dissolving at a rate exceeding most of our current home foreclosures.

What happens when society shares a majority belief, and that belief becomes the accepted norm? Instead of "until death do us part," we might as well substitute "I do . . . at least for now." So what is the reason so many marriages end up in the court system? The most common excuse falls under the heading of "irreconcilable differences," which is nothing more than saying—"I quit."

I believe the move toward divorce is in large part related to one or two trends; the first being that our needs are not being satisfied, the second is our expectations are not being met. As a side note I am not saying divorce is never a warranted course of action. Anytime you are the victim of another's violent or disrespectful behavior, divorce may be your only option based simply on survival.

Kids Say the Darndest Things

So let us dispense with what love *is not* and what love *is* and confer with some leading experts in the field—children. I recently asked a small group of kids, ages four to eight, to define what love means to them. Their answers prove that at times we can learn more from kids then they learn from us.

Karen (age seven) said, "When you love somebody, your eyelashes go up and down, and little stars come out of you."

Jessica (age eight) said, "You really shouldn't say 'I love you' unless you really mean it. But if you mean it, you should say it a lot. People forget."

Emily (age eight) said, "Love is when you kiss all the time. Then when you get tired of kissing, you still want to be together and you talk more. My Mommy and Daddy are like that. They look gross when they kiss."

Chris (age seven) added, "Love is when Mommy sees Daddy smelly and sweaty and still says he is handsomer than Brad Pitt."

And my personal favorite from Nikka (age six), "If you want to learn to love better, you should start with a friend who you hate."

In a letter written by Paul to the Corinthians (13:4–10), love was summed up this way. "Love is patient, love is kind. It does not envy, it does not boast, it is not proud. It is not rude, it is not self-seeking. It is not easily angered, it keeps no record of wrongs. Love does not delight in evil but rejoices with the truth. It always protects, always trusts, always hopes, always perseveres. Love never fails. But where there are prophecies, they will cease; where there are tongues, they will be stilled; where there is knowledge, it will pass away. For we know in part and we prophesy in part, but when perfection comes, the imperfect disappears." This letter from Paul reflects the message of Christ—"to love as I have loved you."

Love Around the World

The true message of love is resonated through every belief system on the planet. The love Christ spoke of so passionately about is a sharp contrast to what we have decided love to mean. We were given our bodies as a physical vehicle to drive through life. We were brought into this world on a given date, and we are going to leave on a given date. Because of this reality, it is difficult to understand the infinite when we all physically begin and end. We came from a place of perfection, love, and grace, and were incarnated into our physical form. But one day we will leave this form and return to where we originated.

Here is a question. If God is perfect love and we were all created in His image, how do we show God we love Him? Is it by how often we sit in church? By how much of the Scriptures we can quote? How about by the number of bumper stickers we have on our car? No, we show our love for God by loving each other unconditionally. Unconditional love means love without attachments, strings or expectations.

All of the spiritual principles in this book are based on a loving altruistic nature. Kindness, forgiveness, and self control will all lead you BACK TO THE SAME PLACE—the place you need to be if you want what you truly desire.

Jesus was love, spoke of its magical splendors and acted in loving ways. We need to copy his blueprint. Do you feel like you do not have enough love? Do you feel a need to run out and chase it? Those of us who have the most love are those who live the life as Jesus did and attract it into our lives. The universe is unfamiliar with love that is about the chase—it only recognizes abundance. Love must continue to grow and not be allowed to die a natural death. Practice the virtues that will cultivate into the things you desire most in life by committing yourself to be a loving person everyday.

Grateful Soul

If the only prayer you say in your entire life is "thank you," that will suffice.
—MEISTER ECKHART (1260–1327)
GERMAN THEOLOGIAN

Two of the most powerful words we can recite to one another are *Thank You*, especially if those spoken words are sincere and truthful. Gratitude is something we should feel for everything we experience, whether for something we have just received, or the wisdom we gain by walking through the fire of some traumatic event.

Staying in a state of gratitude keeps us grounded and humble. I know many people—you may as well—who experience gratitude only when the winds of life are at their back and life seems easy.

The gratefulness they experience is much like a hot shower in that it is short-lived. Life is a magnificent gift that should never be taken lightly. It should be experienced with bewilderment and awe. Yet we know so many who have completely missed the point. They carry around a belief of self-entitlement, feeling as if they are always owed something and rarely, if ever, have any appreciation.

After All Those Years

One of my favorite movies is *Awakenings*, a 1990 film based on an Oliver Sacks memoir. Robert DeNiro plays Leonard Lowe, a catatonic patient lucky enough to survive the 1917–28 encephalitis epidemic.

His attending physician, played by Robin Williams, learned of a new drug called L-Dopa, which was being used in the treatment of Parkinson's disease. He administered it to the patients and found that after decades of being comatose, they were suddenly "awakened."

A few days after his "awakening," Leonard (Robert DeNiro) sat down with the doctor, Malcolm Sayer (Robin Williams) and said, "We have got to tell everybody! We've got to remind them how good it is!" To which Sayer asks, "How good *what* is, Leonard?" Leonard replies, "Read the newspaper, what's it say? All bad, it's all bad. People have forgotten what life is all about. They've forgotten what it's like to be alive! They need to be reminded. They need to be reminded of what they have, what they can lose. What I feel is the joy of life, the gift of life, the freedom of life, the wonderment of life!"

The doctor was able to revive all of the patients from their comatose state, but unfortunately the effect was short-lived. All of the patients ultimately returned to being comatose, regardless of the dosage of L-Dopa that Malcolm administered. Leonard, who was the first to "awaken," also became the first to return to his previous state, forcing all of the other patients to witness what ultimately would be their fate.

Constantly Complaining

One of the strongest points I am trying to drive home in this book is that there really is nothing else to learn; it is about remembering what we have forgotten or have chosen not to practice.

I listen to people all the time speak about the things they are immeasurably grateful for, and then in the next breath complain about what is missing in their lives. Complaining is the antithesis of gratefulness; listening to a complainer can change your disposition very quickly and is among the lowest forms of energy.

I have someone very close in my life who complains all the time; at every turn there is something different to complain about. Complainers usually start out a conversation like this: "I really don't want to sound like I'm complaining, but. . . ."

This person wants you to believe that adding the words "I really don't want to sound like . . ." somehow softens the blow. It acts as some sort of buffer for the listener.

Truth be told, they do like to complain. It is who they are and what they live for, turning trivial matters into something far greater than what they were meant to be. Let me say this, anytime you use the word "but" when communicating with another person, something bad is about to happen. Everything that was said leading up to the word "but" is dismissed. Everything following the word "but" is comprehended, ending up as the real meaning behind what they were trying to say.

I remember my Grandmother was this way every time we went out to dinner. Regardless of what she ordered from the menu, when the dish would arrive it was virtually guaranteed to be sent back. It could have been an exquisite meal prepared by Emeril himself and it would end up back in the kitchen for one reason or another. It was always, "It looks good, but. . . ."

Back to the Beginning

I told the story of my life in the first chapter; I wanted you to understand who I was and what I was before my life-changing event. The idea of me being grateful for anything was right at the bottom, next to compassion.

For the better part of my life I had never experienced gratitude. Not for the people around me trying to help, not for things I had received or had stolen. I never handed out a gift to anyone during holidays or birthdays. It never even occurred to me to send a card and experience gratitude through giving.

For me it was not that I had forgotten what it was like to be grateful; I simply had never felt it. I am here to tell you that there is nothing you can experience that is more powerful than true gratitude; it's something which keeps you humble.

Whenever I needed a place to live, my brother-in-law and sister always took me in. They fed me, put money in my pocket, and asked for nothing in return. In my world, I felt it was owed to me. My brother-in-law married my sister, so he *should* help me out.

Besides not having a place to live, I had no vehicle either. They even offered to loan me the money to purchase a vehicle, at a time when loaning me anything was a dangerous risk—especially if you believed or thought about ever getting the money paid back.

It Kicks In

Eventually, I did end up purchasing a vehicle. I remember a few weeks after picking it up, while on my way to work, I had my first brush with gratitude. I was grateful to have that car, and I was grateful to them for helping me get it.

Following that event, my relationship with them changed. Instead of them asking me to do something, I would offer instead. "What can I do for you, instead of what can you do for me?" I made sure the payments were made on time, just because I was grateful. It was the first time in my life I ever bothered to pay someone back.

When I see someone walking on the shoulder on a busy street, or sleeping under an overpass, I become filled with gratefulness and also compassion, because I know what it feels like.

Today I am grateful I have a home to live in, a nice truck to drive, a publisher who supports my work, and all the magnificence of nature. In short, I am grateful to be alive and share the same air as everything I am connected with.

Better to Give than Receive

One last thought about the car. Not long ago, I purchased a new vehicle and the old one went into the garage. I wanted to keep it as a reminder of my past, but it was also an asset worth five thousand dollars. It was nice having a second car, but did I really need it? Could it be put to a better use? Well, today my sixteen-year-old nephew is driving it.

I gave to him, and at the same time remembered a couple of things. Giving away things we value is very spiritual. Second, in giving there is receiving. I think I was more excited for him to get the car than he was to receive it.

This idea of when we give, we end up receiving, was foreign to me; my idea was when we "take," we receive. Giving to others gives back to us ten-fold to what we offer; the high source emotional reward we receive is second to none. When we give to others, we need to do so without qualification. What that means is that we do not need to remind them of the deed, nor tell them how to use what was given. Giving freely is the same as love in the sense that it must be an unconditional act.

Fourth and One

The way that I understand this spiritual principle is as follows: You need to be grateful for the internal capacity to give freely. A good comparison would be watching the Super Bowl without your home team participating in the game. You can enjoy the game, halftime show, and commercials without having an axe to grind one way or another, and just simply enjoy the fact that you can be in that place.

Gratitude is a feeling of "in this place," the present time, which is the only place we can be. Someone once asked the Buddha,

"Are you God?" "No," he replied. "Are you an angel, then?" "No," he replied again. "What are you then?" they asked. "I am awake." This state of awareness is the only place we can exist, moment to moment, which is really what life is, stringing moments together with moments.

What Are You Grateful For?

Gratitude is often expressed for something we have given or received. We are grateful for our homes, cars, family, and so on, but is that where it ends? I have put together a list of things that I am extremely grateful for. Take time to create one of your own.

1. **Challenges.** Many people do not feel any sense of gratitude for the challenges in their lives, because gratitude is always tied to the niceties of life. I know a person very close to me who is facing a challenge of the life and death variety. It becomes very difficult to act grateful when you are on the receiving end of cancer.

Just as there is a solution to every problem, there is also a solution to every challenge. It is when we emerge from the other side of the flames, and we will, that we understand why this thing happened and what we can take from the experience. Challenges are tests that we all must take, the question is—how many will pass?

2. **Mistakes and Failures.** I put the word "failure" in because we have been conditioned to believe if we do not succeed at something, we have failed. I think the worst thing our educational system

does is use failing grades on a child's report card. Teachers tell the child they have failed, Mom and Dad tell the child they are a failure, and classmates can be especially cruel.

The truth is we never fail at anything; we simply produce a result, which we did not intend. I wonder what would have happened if Thomas Edison or Benjamin Franklin recognized failure as most others do. Mistakes can be one of our best tools, as long as we learn from them.

I certainly remember all of the mistakes I have made in life, BUT I DO NOT IDENTIFY MYSELF WITH THE MISTAKES OF THE PAST. People do the best they can with what they know, with what is available to them. Stay clear of those who want you to feel bad about your mistakes. I say embrace them! Be grateful they occurred, because those mistakes put you in a better place today.

3. Creativity and Emotions. Creativity is one thing we should all have an enormous amount of gratitude for. Through our creative nature we can show people who we are and what we are feeling, through the poetry of the written word, a mesmerizing work of art, or a powerful piece of music.

The works of Michelangelo are breathtaking when you sit and study the work, and it's not hard to appreciate the time and passion that went into each and every piece. I especially enjoy sitting in a dimly lit room listening to *The Phantom of the Opera*. Michael Crawford belts out notes with incredible passion. Creativity is something in all of us, and grateful is the creative soul.

When it comes to gratitude for our emotions, nobody described it better than Jim Valvano—better known to the world as Jimmy V.

At the ESPYs (an awards show sponsored by ESPN), on March 4, 1993, Valvano accepted the Arthur Ashe Award for Courage.

I have listened to many speeches in my day, but nothing has stirred me as emotionally as this one. Here is what Jimmy V. said after being introduced by Dick Vitale: "I'm a very emotional and passionate man. I can't help it. That's being the son of Rocco and Angelina Valvano. It comes with the territory. We hug, we kiss, we love. When people say to me how do you get through life or each day, it's the same thing. To me, there are three things we all should do every day. Number one is *laugh*. You should laugh every day. Number two is *think*. You should spend some time in thought. Number three is, you should have your *emotions moved to tears*, and it could be happiness or joy. Think about it. If you laugh, you think, and you cry, that's a full day. That's a heck of a day. You do that seven days a week, you're going to have something special."

Here is how he closed that night. "I know, I gotta go, I gotta go, and I got one last thing, and I said it before, and I want to say it again. Cancer can take away all my physical abilities. It cannot touch my mind, it cannot touch my heart, and it cannot touch my soul. And those three things are going to carry on forever. I thank you and God bless you all." Jimmy V. died less than two months later, and his speech is regarded as legendary. Jim Valvano is textbook when it comes to having a grateful soul. A person who truly understood and lived his life by the words written in this chapter.

4. Life Itself. Is there a greater gift than life itself? All too often we take this gift for granted; we become consumed with trivial, petty crap that steals the joy we can only experience through life itself.

When we come to a place in our lives where time becomes precious, we then see life through a sense of bewildering awe, where everything is a miracle! Time becomes more precious when there is less of it.

I had a friend who began experiencing slight blurriness in his eyes. He believed his problem could be corrected with glasses, so he made an appointment with an optometrist. He was told he had a degenerative condition, and in a short time he was going to be blind in both eyes.

Everybody was in shock, asking how this could possibly be happening. Well, after a second opinion with another doctor, then a third, his fate had fully been decided. His original diagnosis was not accurate; the second and third found his problem to be a simple eye fungus, easily treatable with medication, and in a few weeks all would be normal again.

He said to me that his attitude toward life is now much different; he is grateful for everything he can see, smell, touch, hear, and feel. What he has a greater appreciation for are the simplest of things, those things we all take for granted.

I would like to close this chapter with the words Robin Williams spoke at the end of the movie *Awakenings.* "It was a season of rebirth for fifteen patients and for us, the caretakers, but now we have to adjust to the realities of miracles. We can hide behind the veil of science and say it was the drug that failed, or the illness itself returned, or that the patients were unable to cope with losing decades of their lives."

"The reality is we don't know anymore about what went wrong than we know what went right. What we do know is, as the chemical window closed, another awakening took place; that the human spirit is more powerful than any drug, and that is what needs to be nourished with work, play, friendship and family."

These are the things that matter, this is what we have forgotten, the simplest things. Although the patients' awakening was brief, and eventually they fell asleep again, they lived that brief period like there was no tomorrow; they felt there was no other option. Always stay awake, stay full of gratitude and reverence, and count every blessing while always being one as well.

Power of Belief

We promise according to our hopes, and we perform according to our fears.
—FRANÇOIS DE LA ROCHEFOUCAULD (1613–80)
FRENCH WRITER

Our ability to believe is the single greatest tool we have to acquire the things we truly desire in life. When our beliefs are inconsistent, we leave our fate in the hands of other people, situations or circumstances. If the course determines the direction, then you must know what it is that you desire most, with unyielding belief that the desire is coming to you. This goes for anything in life, from that job you want, to relationships, to breaking bad habits.

There are laws that govern our universe, just as there are laws in place that govern society. The laws that govern society are broken every minute of every day; the laws of the universe cannot be broken. If you were to fall off a building, the law of gravity says you are going to fall. It does not matter if you are a good person or a bad person, rich or poor, religious or non-religious, you are going to fall, and you are going to hit the ground.

Motivational trainers sometimes use the term, "If you can see it, you can be it!" Sometimes it's true. Every single one of us at some point in our lives will change our beliefs, simply because our earliest beliefs were not our own; they were given to us. This is our introduction to conditioning, which is very different than belief. What I will present to you is where our beliefs come from, why they must change, and what will come to you as a result of shifting your awareness.

All of us live in a universe within the universe; it is called the universe of our minds. This three-pound miracle is capable of creating more than we can imagine even though most of us use less than 10 percent of its full capacity. This is the place where magical things unfold right before your eyes and things you once thought impossible become tangible.

Where Our Beliefs Come From

First, let us look at where our beliefs come from, and why we hold onto beliefs which no longer serve us. That which we hold as truth in our lives is the result of beliefs and fears of the people around us. Who are these people? Usually, these people are the adults, family members, teachers, religious figures, etc., who shape the way we think.

Good or bad, we inherit our beliefs and fears from these people. We are told what we are capable and incapable of doing and the possible consequences when we fail to recognize limitations. We are handed our beliefs of who God is, and what will be the consequences of failing to follow His laws to the absolute letter.

I remember one of my earliest beliefs was that the opposite sex carried cooties. This dreaded disease could be transferred to me simply by touch. Now, as we all know, there is no such thing as cooties; as we experience life, mature, and grow, so does our belief system. Transformation does not allow antiquated ideas to follow.

I was a teenager in the late 1970s. During this period, the country was under the influence of disco. I clearly remember a specific outfit my parents bought me, indicative of the era. Khaki-colored pants with the wide elephant bell bottoms, crushed velvet blazer, a silk shirt with a wide collar, platform shoes, and a gold chain; I was *Stayin' Alive* and wore this outfit whenever I could. I wore it to school, dance halls, weddings, the grocery store, and even to funerals. The problem was, while I continued to grow, the outfit did not. Yet, I continued to wear it. Buttons were falling off; the pant legs were separating at the seams; and finally, the time came for me and my suit to part ways.

Why Our Beliefs Must Change

Holding onto beliefs that no longer serve us only disservice us. Let us take smoking as an example. You see fifteen- and sixteen-year-old kids who believe if they smoke cigarettes they will be cool. For these teens, it's a way of fitting in with a specific group of other teens that share the same belief—their peers. When you get into your twenties, thirties, and forties, the belief of smoking cigarettes to fit in no longer applies, but unfortunately, many continue to smoke. The belief is no longer a belief, a desire to fit in; it's now officially a habit. The action of ingesting a poison into our body is something we want to avoid. For a smoker who wants to break this habit, they will have to change their behavior.

Changing our behavior comes from a fresh set of beliefs forming a vision in our minds. If you see yourself as a non-smoker, but tell yourself it will be impossible to stop, this is an incongruent message. Mind-body-spirit must be in harmony to change our behaviors.

Far too many people use the past as a template for the future. This kind of thinking cripples the magnificence of the soul designed for greatness. Many find it easy to wallow around in discord, finding reasons why things do not work, why your vision will never see fruition.

Which System Do You Operate On?

Your mind is very similar to a computer in how it works. We can even program the mind with the software we choose—anything from high-end operating systems to low-end video games. Remember, the mind runs faster than the most up-to-date computer and has more memory, but if we install the wrong software, does that not affect our performance?

Viruses will render a computer useless. It's the same with our minds. A mind that is contaminated with negative thoughts does not work well. Some people program themselves with the beliefs: "I can't do that!"; "I'm too old to think any differently!"; "I don't have the proper education!"; or, "I'm not that lucky!" This litany of negative thinking is sent out into the universe, crippling our spiritual soul.

Remember, what we focus on becomes our reality, so the universe gives us exactly what we ask of it. The role of the victim is one vision that will keep us down for sure. Aligning ourselves with labels and excuses keeps us in a negative state of mind. We label ourselves based on our past experiences and use these labels to create excuses for ourselves. Excuses like: "My father beat me when I was a child"; "My mother wasn't there for me"; "I was bullied my whole life"; "My spouse cheated on me"; "I can't trust anyone."

It's all tough stuff, but guess what? We all have a story to tell. We all face challenges; the tough stuff is part of life. But there must come a time when you ask yourself, "Is the past going to rule me, or will I rule my past?" By taking charge of the past, you shift your awareness and improve your state of mind. We all have this ability, but too many of us fail to use it.

Awareness Shift

Undoing negative conditioning is not easy, but by shifting our awareness and creating a connection of mind-body-spirit, you can operate from the highest part of your being. It says in the Scriptures "Through God, all things are possible" (Matthew 19–26). Belief in anything that we want to attract into our lives starts by believing in the God that created us.

Today more than ever, part of the treatment process for any disease is the belief in the cure. Medicine recognizes the power of mind-body-spirit (*along with medications and diet*), and gives a person the best chance for a full recovery.

A placebo is the perfect example. A placebo is a pill that contains no medicinal value and is based solely on the power of suggestion. The patient is told the pill will be all that is needed to facilitate a cure. It is this belief, not the pill itself, which makes the person feel better.

Today, belief works hand-in-hand with modern medicine. I do not endorse the idea that if your condition could ultimately lead to death, that belief alone will carry you through—medical care is required as well. I remember watching a news program where a child was very ill and the parents would not allow physicians to treat her. Instead, they relied only on prayer. The child eventually died and the parents attributed her death to God's will. The judicial system, however, disagreed.

Just Visiting

There is a great story about illness and belief that I will share with you. A minister noticed that a woman in his congregation had not been attending services for quite some time. She was an elderly woman, so the minister decided to take a drive to her home, which was located approximately forty miles from the church. He arrived at the woman's house and knocked on the door. The woman opened the door and was surprised to see the minister at her home. She invited him in. As they sat talking, the woman offered to serve some refreshments. The minister said that would be nice, so she went to the kitchen to prepare some tea and get some cookies.

While the woman was in the kitchen, the minister looked around the living room at the beautiful antiques, pottery, and Victorian furniture. The piece that really caught his eye was a beautiful pipe organ in the corner, magnificently displayed with the pipes running up the wall. As the minister got closer, he noticed a bowl of water on the organ. Floating in the water was a condom. The minister was flabbergasted. The woman was returning back to the living room, so he darted back to his seat, not wanting to embarrass her. The two enjoyed their time together, having a snack, and sharing a nice conversation. The time came for the minister to leave. He got up from his chair, thanked the woman for her hospitality, and began walking towards the front door when he stopped and turned around. Piqued with curiosity, he pointed at the bowl and asked, "What is that?"

"Oh, that!" she replied. "Well, that is just a miracle."

"What do you mean, a miracle?" the minister wondered.

"Well, I am in my nineties you know, and last fall I was very ill. Many thought I was going to die. One day while I was out walking, I came across a package. So I bent down and picked it up, then read the instructions. It said for the prevention of disease, moisten and place on your organ. I haven't been sick one day since then!"

So, as you can see, it is all about what you believe.

A Tiny Place in Scotland

In 1962 a woman named Eileen Caddy, her husband Peter, and Dorothy MacLean created the Findhorn Foundation, located in Scotland. Today, the Findhorn Foundation is recognized world-wide as one of the finest spiritual communities in existence. On the subject of belief, Eileen Caddy said, "The secret to making something work in your lives is first of all, the deep desire to make it work; then the faith and belief it can work; then hold that clear definite vision in your consciousness and see it working out step by step, without one thought of doubt or disbelief."

Another universal law is what Caddy calls the **Law of Attraction**. It is a law that many choose to ignore. Too many people base what their future holds on their failed expectations and on what others tell them. We look back at our past, and for many of us, the past is messy. We see what we believe are failures. The truth is, you never fail at anything. Instead, you only attract a result. The result you attract may not have been the one you hoped for, but still you produced a result.

In the physical world we see all kinds of limits and resistance. I do not want to get too philosophical here, but I want to talk about this briefly. In our physical form, we enter this world and then at some point in time we leave this world—but we never die.

The human experience is a grand paradox—we die and yet we live forever. In our present form we see ourselves as human beings, finite in what we can create for ourselves and for others. We use our minds in a manner that creates very little in terms of high energy, but high levels of low source energy. When we operate from our true self, our spiritual self, the mind does not recognize limitations. The mind does not recognize low energy states, because it is not programmed to understand anything except a world of abundance, a world without limitations, and a world without end.

Everything in the universe is connected. We are spiritual beings living a human experience instead of human beings living a spiritual experience. When you see your life from this perspective, everything becomes available to you immediately, regardless of what you have done or where you have been. When you make this shift, you trust in the creative power of God and the universe becomes yours in which to play. This connection of mind-body-spirit can and will bring to you all that you desire if you simply take the time to hold that vision.

❧

A New Vision

Begin to be now what you will be hereafter.
—WILLIAM JAMES (1842–1910)
PSYCHOLOGIST AND PHILOSOPHER

William James is considered one of the great thinkers of the nineteenth century. In 1890 James wrote *The Principles of Psychology*, which is still valued today. James was pragmatic in thought. He was concerned with results rather than theories. He was also manic-depressive, or what we refer to today as bipolar.

Although he was diagnosed manic depressive, he still managed to write and teach without Prozac—pretty amazing when you think about it. On the subject of mind imagery, James said, "There is a law in psychology that if you form a picture in your mind of what you would like to be, and you hold that picture long enough, you will soon become exactly what you have been thinking." Good or bad, right or wrong, the universe will deliver exactly what you desire the most.

Flying through Space

The universe does not decide what is good or bad, only what you put out. An example of this misguided belief took place on March 26, 1997, in a home located near the city of San Diego. Thirty-nine people were found dead. Each of the deceased was dressed alike. All wore black outfits, black gym shoes, a unique logo, and they all had the same amount of currency in their pockets. Lying on bunk beds, each person had a plastic bag securely fastened over their face and head. Later it was discovered, through toxicology testing, that all had ingested a lethal cocktail mixture prior to suffocating themselves.

Marshall Applewhite, one of the founders of Heaven's Gate, believed along with thirty-eight others that behind the comet Hale-Bopp was another comet carrying Jesus Christ. The belief was that the planet Earth was about to be recycled and the only chance of survival was to leave the physical plane immediately. At one point, they lived in a home of total darkness to get a feeling of what they would experience on their long journey through outer space. The universe does not decide right or wrong, only what you believe and attract.

Puttin' on the Pounds

There was a period in my life when my weight went from a healthy 195 pounds to 227 pounds. I always thought of myself as a physically fit athlete. Seeing myself in the mirror, I saw what I had become.

Remember, just because we are not where we want to be right now, does not mean our circumstances will remain unchanged. The present condition is just that. The person I was looking at and the person I remembered were not the same. My desire was to regain my healthy self, which I started to do that day.

I went to my kitchen, tossing out all the foods and snacks that I believed were unhealthy. The cupboards were completely bare. Once I emptied out all the carryout containers and chocolate bars, the refrigerator, much like the cupboard shelves, became empty. The next thing I did was obtain a membership at a well-known fitness club.

I have heard the argument, "Why spend money on a health club when you can just as easily put equipment in the house?" My answer to that is environment. It is important for me to go to a training facility where I am surrounded by others actively engaged in some form of exercise, and where the environment makes the investment well worth it. Besides, I have been in many homes where I have seen weight-lifting equipment or treadmills used as clothes hangers or dust catchers.

I immediately began by filling my refrigerator with a variety of fruits and vegetables. I bought cartons of yogurt and the necessary vitamin supplements. I was determined at that moment that my transformation would begin.

The following morning I began the day in typical fashion by showering, talking with God, and making my bed. When I opened the refrigerator and saw all that healthy food, I thought to myself, "There's nothing here to eat." I had no interest in eating the healthy food I had just purchased twelve hours before. Instead, I joined a friend at a local restaurant for my usual unhealthy breakfast. I returned home, wrote for a while, and did not go to that well-known fitness club that I had just purchased a membership at to exercise.

Truth be told, my unhealthy behaviors continued for some time, and so did the vision I held of myself. I cannot begin to tell you how much food I threw out at the end of each week, only to go back to the same store and repurchase the exact same items. And how many times did I go to the fitness center to exercise during the first ninety days that I had that membership? You got it—Zero!

Still, I had the desire to change myself. I had the desire William James talked about to "keep that picture long enough." Because I remained steadfast, I began acting in ways to support my vision. I started out every morning eating a healthy breakfast, filling my body with supplements and nutrition. I continue to do so today. Now, each day, I spend an hour or two at my local health club. Do I ever go outside the program? Of course I do, but not nearly as much as I used to.

If your vision is strong enough and held clearly in your mind without any disbelief, then your behavior will align with your vision. My vision of better health actually changed my belief about how long I needed to sleep in order to feel rested. There was a time when I believed I needed seven, eight, or even nine hours of sleep each night. Now, I require maybe five hours a night to feel rested and energized, because my health has improved. When you're overweight and out of shape, under stress and anxious, you need more sleep.

When your vision is strong enough, you can use that vision to change anything; its application goes far beyond just losing weight.

116

I applied my new vision to how I deal with other people, including family, friends, and strangers. I used to be very quick to judge others, looking for the worst, trying to find some hidden agenda. Maybe you are like this, or maybe know someone who is.

Operating from this perspective will only attract the people you are asking to attract. When you can see another human being as you see yourself, you cannot help but shift your awareness in how you treat others. In arguments and disputes among friends, family or co-workers, the unease usually arises from one person needing to be right and proving another wrong. The truth is that no one is 100 percent correct and no one is 100 percent wrong. Each person contributes either directly or indirectly to any situation. When you accept that, judgments and confrontation are replaced with kindness and cooperation.

How Much Work Does It Take?

Carlos Castaneda once said, "We either make ourselves miserable, or we make ourselves strong. The amount of work is the same." Making your vision come to fruition requires work and a positive, steadfast approach.

If you constantly say to yourself, "I do not have what it takes"; or, "I am not smart enough"; or, "I haven't had the breaks you've had"; then you will fail in your vision. Of course, it takes a lot of effort to be so negative. Yes, it takes a lot of work to be miserable. You end up fighting with your thoughts against everything available to you in a world full of abundance. Remember what it says in the Scriptures: "As man thinketh so is he" (Proverbs 23:7).

In order to acquire the things we truly desire in life, we must believe in ourselves and undo the negative thoughts and labels that we have accumulated over time. We must align our behaviors to our visions. To achieve this, I have included five ideas to reflect on as you go through this manifestation process.

1. Exercise Patience. The single greatest champion of any vision we have for ourselves is patience. Most of us tend to lack patience. In the absence of patience, anything worth waiting for will never see fruition. Willpower is not patience, and willpower is what we tend to reach for to fill the space between what we desire and the realization of that desire.

If your desire is to lose twenty pounds, see yourself as already there. Keep in mind it took some time to gain the additional weight, so it will also take some time to lose it. We tend to quit what we are doing because the desired result does not arrive in lightning speed. It is a convenient reason to abort.

On magazine covers there is often a person smiling and holding a pair of pants appearing five- to ten-sizes too large and inside the magazine is a program for losing twenty pounds in twenty days. Check out the fine print. At the bottom of the ad is that disclaimer, "results not typical." Yet people still spend the money for the magic fix. The last time I checked, weight loss was achieved by burning more calories than you take in. You also have to eat properly and exercise.

The reason people buy into the quick fix is because they see a fast way to lose weight with little effort. After all, why do something difficult when there is an easier option?

I would suggest you don't read magazines that promote accelerated weight loss. Pay no attention to the commercials pushing pills to lose weight, and avoid getting on the scale ten times a day. Choose a sensible program built on diet and exercise. Most of all make patience a part of the program.

2. Manage Your Emotions. The best way to know if what you are doing is right for you is to gauge your feelings. How does what you are doing make you feel? If what you are doing has you feeling uninspired, it is time to reassess what you are doing, or the way you are going about it.

A feeling of discontent tells you that you are moving in a direction that is taking you further from inner happiness. Experiencing discontent or lack of satisfaction only brings more of the same. To draw the good into your life, you have to be happy and joyful. You have to feel good. By maximizing your mental potential with your emotional potential, anything is achievable.

3. Gratitude. Being grateful is not only offering thanks for what is coming; it is offering thanks for what we already have. The human side of gratitude comes from receiving something good, something that is a tangible asset. Many people only experience gratitude when the wind is at their backs and everything they touch turns to gold.

This feeling of self-entitlement is dangerous because it lacks humility. Nobody deserves anything in this world unless they are willing to put forth the effort to obtain it. Throughout a good part of my life I have experienced many negative results. My problems, in turn, created far greater problems for other people.

I know what it is like to be dead broke emotionally, spiritually, and financially. I know what it feels to live in a dumpster—that was my home in Westminster, California. I know what it feels like when your spouse throws you out of your home with nothing but the clothes on your back. Whatever you have experienced, I can promise you I have probably been there.

Not too long ago, someone said, "It must feel great to finally be getting ahead in life and shoving everyone's nose in it." I am equally as grateful for all the good I have in my life, as well as all the bad I have experienced in life, and I would not change it for the world. It has been said that living well is the best revenge. I say, living well is having a grateful soul for all you have endured and celebrated.

4. Write It Down. I encourage you to keep a journal. A journal is a powerful tool in monitoring your progress and managing your feelings. The pen is mightier than the sword. When it comes to managing emotions, especially negative emotions, journaling is the best way to get back into a resourceful state of mind. A person needs thirty minutes, at least, to calm down from an experience that causes them anger.

Writing allows you to work through the situation, telling the other party what they have done, how you feel about it, and a possible resolution to the situation. Once you've written down your feelings, place the letter in an envelope and plan to mail it the following day. Ninety-nine percent of the time your letter will go into the garbage rather than in the mailbox.

Each evening before I go to bed I write down, in order, what I will accomplish the following day. I have found that when I write out what I will do, 90 percent of it is accomplished. When I do not write it down, less than 40 percent of what I want to do gets done. Keep a daily journal of all that you expect to do and update it every evening.

5. Be Dialed In. Keep the vision in front of you and realize obstacles are a part of life. I think some of the greatest obstacles that you will encounter are your relatives. This was the case in my life and probably yours as well. You will hear a litany of reasons why you are being foolish, why you cannot reach your goals, and you'll hear all about your past failings.

We never fail at anything. We always produce some result. Failing in life is when you come to a point where you see yourself as useless. Many times in my life I have heard the same things about what I can or cannot do based on previous attempts. This is annoying, especially when the words are coming from those that you love. I have a member of my family who loves to give advice, even when I do not request it. This relative is an example of the type of person who not only knows what is best for them, but what is best for everyone else, including me. What they offer is rarely in your best interest. I know.

If I listened to the advice of my "helpful" relatives, my career would have been in retail. Offer people who are giving free advice a kind "thank you" or "I never thought about it that way," but never let them shape a vision for you. Keep yourself dialed in by always holding onto your vision.

Take some time every day to create your perfect day and incorporate all your senses when doing these exercises. As I close out this chapter, I want you to remember who you are. You are in collaboration with the God that created you; there is unlimited power within this force. You are a magnificent part of the whole, engineered for greatness! If you are going to be a slave, be a slave to your beliefs.

❧

Art of Self-Control

In one way or another, we are all in a wheelchair.
—JIM MACLAREN
LIFE MENTOR, COACH

In 1985 Jim MacLaren was doing his undergraduate work at Yale University, studying theater. He was also a member of the football team, stunningly handsome, and 6′5″, 300 pounds. Following a late theater rehearsal one day in the fall, he was riding his motorcycle around New York City, thinking of the evening as "full of possibilities." The next thing Jim MacLaren remembers was waking up in Bellevue Hospital eight days later.

The "evening of possibilities" ended when Jim was struck by a forty thousand pound city bus. He was initially presumed dead, and his body was chalked out before being transported. Once at the hospital, after realizing he was still alive, it took eighteen hours of surgery to stabilize him, and a decision was made to amputate his left leg below the knee.

During his rehabilitation he began swimming and developed an interest in triathlons. Not only was he able to reshape his body for the rigors of these events, he went on to become the fastest one-legged endurance runner in the world, setting records in some very grueling races, including the New York City Marathon and the Ironman Triathlon in Hawaii. Jim MacLaren was consistently out-distancing 80 percent of the athletes he competed with who had the use of both legs, and he felt he was "back in it, back in the game of life."

Lightning Strikes Twice

In June of 1993, two miles into the bike leg of an event in California, Jim MacLaren's life was about to take another turn. Racing on a closed course, a traffic marshal did not properly gauge MacLaren's speed, allowing a truck to drive through the intersection. The truck struck the rear wheel of his bicycle, hurling him head first into a sign post, breaking his neck.

Once again finding himself in a hospital, his attending physician told him he was a quadriplegic and he would never move or feel anything from the chest down for the rest of his life. A friend from college was visiting when MacLaren said, "Ya' know, I don't know if I can do this again."

Doctors certainly can give us a prognosis based on our injuries, but have no way of determining the long range outcome of the human spirit. It took thousands of hours of exhaustive rehabilitation, devout commitment and belief, but Jim MacLaren did end up gaining some motor function and all sensation back as well. In his words, he "planted a seed in his garden of hope" and was rewarded.

His doctors called him a "living miracle," but somehow I do not see him thinking of himself that way. He knew his mind was stronger than his body. Today, Jim MacLaren is the creator of the **Choose Living Foundation** and a highly sought-after motivational speaker. He has been featured on the Jim Rome radio show and appeared as a guest with Oprah Winfrey. He was even presented the Arthur Ashe Courage Award at the 2005 ESPY awards. In Jim's own words, "It's a journey . . . a journey about living with adversity." And I think you would be hard-pressed to find a person who has handled adversity better than Jim MacLaren.

Now, your personal ability to conquer adversity does not have to be quite this dramatic—it is the end result, that is really all that matters. It is true when Jim MacLaren said, "One way or another we are all in a wheelchair."

Today I'll Become an Addict

I always tell people that nobody wakes up one day and says to themselves, "It's a great day to become an addict—today is the day I'll start to destroy my life." Events show up in the introductory part of life, and then rear their ugly heads in the later stages. As I have already stated, "There is nothing in the external world that can provide you with peace, if the internal self is incongruent."

We have seen many souls engage in this type of chase; you may know someone in your life engaged in a struggle with an addiction, someone in their own "wheelchair." But the end result is always the same; the chase through an addictive lifestyle never ends in the positive. When you see yourself as dependent, you will live like it, along with all the destructive low energy emotions associated with that dependency. It is a very dark, masochistic existence. There is nothing worse a person can believe about themselves, or hear from a loved one, than that they are useless and totally incapable of doing anything useful or contributory in society.

I am not a psychiatrist, psychologist, or therapist. I have struggled with many things over a large part of my adult life, and I am very open about this fact. These challenges prepared me for the work I am blessed to do today. I know what this world is like; it is pure insanity when seen through the eyes of an addict. And trying to find a way out of the "wheelchair" can be quite challenging.

Program, Get Your Program

Encouraged by many to try, I found twelve-step programs were just not for me. The closest I ever came to a truly effective treatment was when I lost my freedom for a spell in a county jail.

I will be the first to applaud anyone successful in one of these programs and I wish you only continued success in your marvelous work. For me, however, that is how I saw these programs—as a lot of work. Meetings twice a day, checking in with other people, having mentors, all became more and more work.

I knew I wanted my behavior to change, but I was not looking for a second job. Besides, all the things I was addicted to would have had me in meetings nearly every waking hour. Addictions for me personally were like two magnets. All I needed was to get close and they came instantly together. My consciousness at that time was one of an ego-centered existence, and putting ego and addiction together became the perfect storm.

Now, I do want to make one thing perfectly clear—I am not saying or even mildly suggesting support programs do not work; they do. I have many friends who have gone through them and are alive and well because of these programs.

Why Ask Why?

Thinking from ego is the way not to find the answers you're thinking about. Why was I broke? Why was I a thief? Why am I a con? Why am I homeless? Why are my friends and family avoiding me? Why are my clothes so filthy? You can come up with all kinds of questions, people to blame, but never the truthful answer. Like most addicts, I never liked being told what to do. This is how addictions treat us; they tell us what to do and when to do it. What they do not tell us is—WHEN TO STOP.

When in the throws of an addiction, your ego is always there to back you up. To admit you are powerless in this fight is very difficult; being powerless means setting aside your ego, and going back to who you once were. In the Scripture it says, "With God all things are possible" (Matthew 19:26). *If You Only Knew What You Already Know*, tells us to return to those possibilities.

127

In the process of returning, you shed the ego, the fake identity, and begin the process of a new awareness. Like I said, you do not wake up one day and declare you are going to be an addict. It is a process of putting certain properties into your body, or thoughts, and images into your mind over a long period of time. The good news is that the return flight is much more enjoyable.

Hitting the Piñata

Recently, I was watching a sporting event on television. When the game went to a commercial, I started flipping through the channels and stopped at what looked like an interesting program. It dealt with people in the throws of some sort of addictive behavior.

I watched as one of the family members came in through the front door and walked into the family room. He was greeted by family, friends, lights, and cameras—it was clearly a "made for TV" ambush. This person became agitated. Then out of nowhere he was bombarded with low source verbiage. "Do you know how much pain you are causing us?" "You weren't raised this way!" "You're destroying everyone around you!"

Every person surrounding the surprised victim had the opportunity to express what they were going through as a result of the behavior of this person. Our human piñata sat silently in a state of shock as the assault continued.

This type of therapy cannot be viewed as positive. If the goal is to elevate the consciousness of the addicted soul, guilt and shame are not the constructive course of action. This type of therapy will only reinforce what that person already believes about themselves. Johann Wolfgang von Goethe once said, "If you treat an individual as he is, he will stay as he is; but if you treat him as if he were what he ought to be and could be, he will become what he ought to be and could be." The goal should always be for a person to see himself or herself as what they "ought to be and could be."

William James reminded us that, "If we hold a picture in our minds long enough, that is exactly what we will become in reality." When we use negative therapy to reach someone, as this television show was doing, we assist in developing that picture. This will almost certainly drive the person deeper into their destructive ways.

Take the Over/Under

I can remember weekends during football season as being a stressful time in my home—my gambling made it that way. Like most people that gamble, I was usually on the losing end of the bet and would always rely on a winning streak to keep me in the game. If I lost money Saturday, no problem; I had NFL games on Sunday. If I lost on Sunday, there was always the night game on Monday to make it up.

You have probably heard of cases where gamblers ended up losing every penny they had. They mortgaged their house, went through the kid's college fund, and begged and borrowed from everyone they knew. They never felt a reason to stop because they were just one hand, one roll of the dice, or one game away from getting it all back.

The end result for gamblers is the loss of friends, family, job, and in the worst cases, when feeling completely hopeless—loss of life. This is the insanity of a gambling addiction. In my particular case I had to steal money before my wife discovered it was missing. The NSF notices from the bank told a story I could not. Trying to shame me to stop gambling only convinced me to gamble more. Telling me I was a liar, a rotten husband, and a loser did nothing but reinforce what I already believed about myself.

Unspoken Addictions

Addictions come in all shapes and sizes, and it is difficult to measure the grip on the individual based solely on the impact the addiction has on society. There are addictions that consume people every waking minute, like crack and heroin. There are also addictions to abusive behavior, both physically and mentally, which often diminish a person's self-worth.

Rarely, if ever, is spiritual abuse dealt with, and it may be kind to call it spiritual abuse. It's more like people we trust as spiritual advisors—be they priests or religious leaders, who use God and fear to satisfy their own compulsions.

We don't need to go into graphic detail; the media has done a good job of taking care of that recently with well-publicized stories on the Catholic Church and polygamist sects. But even when the issue is brought to light, it is not dealt with appropriately. It sometimes just seems easier to throw money at the problem to make it go away than to deal with it head on.

You may be asking yourself—what is the difference between addiction and compulsion? In my opinion, addiction and compulsion go hand in hand, and are not worth splitting hairs over, but I do believe they are equal in their destructive nature. Compulsive behavior and anything we repeat every day ultimately can become addictive.

Perverted Tendencies

Another addictive behavior that has remained silent, but is proving to be a real problem in society, is sexual addictions. The question arises, how can a natural act between two people be construed as addictive? One of the reasons this problem has never really been addressed properly is because the desire for sex is normal, whereas the desire for drugs and alcohol are considered poor choices made by the addict and considered socially acceptable.

When someone is in the throws of a sexual addiction, they no longer see a partner as a partner; they see them as an object. Sex with control and domination is what the ego feeds off of. As we have discussed previously, we chase after love because we believe we do not have enough. We chase after what we think will make us happy, or believe we need.

Just as the person addicted to drugs, alcohol, or gambling is searching for relief, the same holds true for the person addicted to sex. They attempt to fill an inner void with the greatest of external pleasures. People addicted to crack cocaine never achieve the same high as they reached the first time the drug entered their lungs. The euphoria is a feeling of complete and total exhilaration—a feeling, however, that can never be duplicated again, regardless of the amount ingested.

Sex addiction acts much the same; the addict must act on other sexual behaviors to find another first experience all over again. This addiction is one our society is oblivious to, because in the grand scheme of our existence, sex is a normal act. Just as the alcoholic who needs a double, the sexually addicted needs heightened acts of false pleasure. Pornography is an issue that society needs to deal with; this perversion is something we have kept in the basement far too long, pretending it does not exist.

Anything that consumes our thought process and actions to the point of robbing us of our freedom cannot be good. The penchant behind these acts is dominance, a feeling of power and control. Controlled substance abuse begins with an occasional drink, snorting a line, or swallowing a pill. The next thing you know, what you once had control of, now has control of you.

People with perverted tendencies tend at first to just dabble in it. As the need grows, the tendencies become consuming. Graphically the need intensifies, especially with the access people have through the Internet. After some time, watching it on a screen will no longer suffice. This is when the fantasy needs to be acted out with an object; a person you are willing to dehumanize.

The magic of romance and feelings of intimacy are replaced with impulses of raw sex. The love for a spouse is exchanged for sexual dominance over another. There have been stories where the fear of exposure, coupled with overwhelming feelings of shame, have led to loss of life. I learned of a man who was dismissed from his job because of viewing pornographic images on his computer. He did all he could to come to grips with his addiction, but the guilt became too overwhelming. He found the best way to deal with his problem was to step out in front of a speeding train. Addictions are that powerful.

Seeing the Light

The only way to change any behavior is for a person to change how they see themselves. I personally do not believe therapy, counseling, or learning coping mechanisms is the answer. But, I also do not have any problem with people who do. When we change the way we see things, the things we see will change. People will go anywhere, anyplace, to get answers to what troubles them.

Returning back to our spiritual self is different—*If You Only Knew What You Already Know.* Freeing ourselves from any addictive pattern comes from the work we do internally, seeing who we truly are, and where we originated from. This has nothing to do with religion; this has everything to do with returning to a state of grace from where we all came—there is no altar required.

It has been said that when you find yourself in a hole, the last thing you want to do is keep digging. You can get yourself out of any addiction you find yourself in—I am living proof of this and know it to be true. The people around you can provide you with the shovels to dig more, or you can connect to our Creator and ask him to throw you a rope and pull you from the depths of your own personal hell.

Born Again

It is when we return that life is new again, meaning we are free to experience it the way we once did. Stocks and bonds have an inverse relationship, meaning as the value of one rises, the other falls, and vice-versa. It is the same when we overcome an addiction. As we regain our lives free of addictions, we rise above and beyond all limitations, and those darkened days drop. Why would anyone want to return to a state of darkness after reclaiming their own magnificence!

There is no greater accomplishment for you to master, and the Master is the only way. So you ask— "Is all that I need to do is ask for this addiction to be taken from me?" No. There is a great deal of work that you must do yourself. God knows what is in the hearts and minds of all of us. You can lie to friends, family, and co-workers but not to yourself or God. You must be ready to make that change, because one way or another, "we are all in a wheelchair."

You Are What You Eat

A wise man should consider that health is the greatest of human blessings.
—HIPPOCRATES (CA. 460 BC–CA. 370 BC)
ANCIENT GREEK PHYSICIAN

So far we have discussed how to strengthen ourselves in terms of how we live our lives by living through specific and deliberate actions. In this chapter, I would like to discuss strengthening ourselves through specific and deliberate actions as they relate to our bodies.

A proper diet is critical to maintaining optimal health for these physical vessels God has uniquely assigned to each one of us. These steps are not only critical, but spiritual. What I would like to attempt to answer here are some of the questions I have been asked about this subject in the past.

Questions like: Why don't people finish what they started? What is the best way to diet? What foods are best to eat? My goal is to provide you with enough information to encourage you to look at what you are doing or not doing and most importantly, to show you why diet is so vital to maintaining a proper lifestyle.

I am not a doctor or nutritional expert. I have, however, studied the subject a great deal and live the life. Therefore, I do feel qualified to speak on the subject. Before I go on, I would add that my advice should not be substituted for medical advice, and ask that you seek out a medical professional before starting any diet program.

It's Easy When You Have To

The next time you are in line at the grocery store, take a look at the magazines on the rack near the checkout. I would be willing to bet a large percentage of what you see in front of you is related to weight loss. You know the covers I'm talking about. There is a thin person two or three sizes bigger then they are now. They are holding a pair of pants away from their now thin body, grinning widely while they exclaim the virtues of what this new diet has done for them.

On television it is more of the same type of advertising, with disclaimers at the end of each spot stating the obligatory "results not typical" and "this (product) must be used in conjunction with proper diet and exercise."

Dieting and eating sensibly have come to have the same meaning, even though the two share different definitions. For many Americans, dieting is something one is forced to do. When we go through a good chunk of our life eating whatever we choose to eat, then for some health reason are put on a diet, this switch can be difficult to deal with.

A person I know has thyroid cancer, which forces him every year to go on a low-iodine diet as part of the treatment. Put simply,

for a few weeks a year he must omit all food that contains iodine—
which just happens to include all seafood, dairy products (milk,
cheese, cream, yogurt, butter, etc.), eggs, commercial baked goods,
(bread, cakes, crackers, donuts, cookies, etc.), chocolate, soy products,
restaurant food, fast food, and just about everything found in a grocery
store that is manufactured or processed. He calls it the "oatmeal and
lettuce diet." People ask him how can he can do it, but it is amazing
what dietary changes you can make when you have no choice.

Just the Facts

We hear so often about the rising cost of health care. If people would
just start taking preventive measures, we would see a sharp decline
in the health care system costs. I want to share some rather disturbing facts on weight gain thanks to the web site obesityinamerica.org.

1. Obesity is the second leading cause of preventable death in
the United States.

2. Approximately 127 million adults in the United States are
overweight; another 60 million are obese.

3. Currently, an estimated 65.2 percent of adults in the United
States aged twenty and older and 15 percent of children and adoles-
cents are overweight, and 30.5 percent are obese.

4. An estimated 400,000 deaths in the United States per year
may be attributed to poor diet and low physical activity.

5. It has been estimated that the annual cost of being over-weight and obese in the United States is $122.9 billion. This estimate accounts for $64.1 billion in direct costs and $58.8 billion in indirect costs related to the obesity epidemic.

So how do you know if you are considered overweight or obese? This is done by combining your height and weight and coming up with your Body Mass Index (BMI). This index indicates if you are overweight, obese, underweight, or normal. You can obtain your BMI by going to www.bmi-calculator.net.

If your BMI is between 17 and 22 you will have a longer life expectancy. If your BMI is be between 23 and 25 you are considered in the normal range. Anything above 25 is considered overweight and over 30 is considered obese, putting you at far greater risk for heart disease, high blood pressure, and other serious health problems.

Video Games Are Not Exercise

Our society recognizes a trim body as beautiful and successful. Because of computer and video games, children in this country are far less active than children from previous generations. I have talked to parents from other cultures who say their children are not allowed to sit timelessly in front of the computer. Their belief is that children need to be active, using their hands and their minds.

As I said earlier, there are hundreds of diet plans, programs, and group meetings out there promising something very few will accomplish. I was on a diet once where I lost ten pounds in seven days; it was called the flu. The last time I checked, weight loss occurs when we burn more calories than we take in. Did you know that just taking a few inches off of your waistline will greatly reduce your risk for all types of health issues!

Dieting is not about the newest flavor of the week; it requires a lifelong commitment. Let us take a look at our choices, what would be better, and finally lay out some points that you may find helpful.

I'll Have a #3 Biggie Sized to Go

So what do we eat? This is another area in which we already know right from wrong, but fail to practice. We use convenience and lack of time as the biggest excuse. It is much easier to blast through a drive-thru then it is to prepare a sensible breakfast or lunch. I usually eat five meals per day instead of the traditional three. What I have found is by eating smaller portions, I am more energized and my insulin levels remain stable throughout the day.

Breakfast should never be passed up; this meal gets the metabolism going as well as brain function. Some will argue this is the most important meal of the day, but I have heard the same arguments for lunch and dinner. I think if we treat them all equally, and remember to break them into five smaller meals, we will tend to eat healthier all day.

The question is: What do we normally eat to get our day started? What we usually opt for is counterproductive to the purpose of why we eat breakfast. Children will have sugar-laced bowls of cereal with

139

very little nutritional value and a glass of orange juice, and become hungry a couple of hours later. Or we choose the pancakes, bacon, potatoes, and toast combo platter, and shortly thereafter experience the "carb-crash."

Breakfast Suggestions

Before your feet touch the ground in the morning and you begin to think about breakfast, take time to say a quick prayer and think of at least five things you are grateful for. This is a great way for getting in a good frame of mind before you start your day.

I personally choose to drink my breakfast each morning. If you do not have a Magic Bullet™ blender or own a juicer, I would encourage you to purchase one. They are wonderful for preparing healthy drinks. I take a banana, strawberries, blueberries, six ounces of yogurt, and add this into the blender. I then add a little granola, skim milk, ice cubes, and it makes for one very healthy drink. Additionally, I may grab a bowl of oatmeal or cold cereal, which sustains me until my next meal two hours later.

I also like to take a full complement of supplements and chase them down with a glass of grape juice. A good frame of mind, a healthy breakfast, all the essential vitamins and minerals, and I would say that this is one heck of way to start your day. As I said earlier, I believe it to be smarter eating every couple of hours, four or five times a day in smaller portions, because it keeps our metabolism working properly and insulin levels in check.

Beware of the Mascot

You will hear the pros and cons of supplements debated frequently. Some say they are not necessary because we get them in the foods we eat. Some say they are necessary because our soil has been depleted of vitamins and minerals. Still others claim people who smoke, drink coffee in excess, abuse alcohol, and live a life of stress will lose vitamins at a more rapid pace, so they need to supplement.

I see nothing wrong in taking supplements and believe they are a good insurance policy. I would suggest, however, staying away from the meal replacement shakes, energy and sports drinks that claim to replenish lost vitamins and minerals. Many are laced with unnecessary sugar, empty calories, and become counterproductive.

Eating right goes along with what this book is about; it is not learning what to eat, it is remembering what we should eat, because old habits die hard. This means eating abundant amounts of all varieties of fresh fruits and vegetables. If eating greens raw, such as broccoli, spinach, and other types is not for you, steam them. When you boil them, you extract exactly what you are trying to keep in — the nutrients.

Sensible eating is avoiding places with the smiling mascots. You know the redheaded clown, large-headed king, the girl with the pigtails, and the southern gentleman in the finely tailored white suit.

Although some fats found in foods are essential, you will not find them in styrofoam containers; you will find them in avocados, raw nuts, seeds, and olive oil. Grabbing a value meal for many is tasty and quick, but a sandwich high in trans-fat, greasy fries, and a sugary soda should be eliminated completely.

Eating sensibly means choosing our best options at every meal; I would suggest to you that for lunch it is best to keep it light. I hear people often say at suppertime they are a "meat and potatoes" person. Meat and potatoes are not a good combination of foods to digest, not to mention the fats in the meat, or the butter or gravy that accompany the potatoes. If you are going to eat a steak, then eat a steak. Mix the meal with a salad and good multi-grain bread. My advice for a meal at dinner time is the same, keep it light!

Junk Food Is Not a Food Group

When the potato chip makers created the slogan "no one can eat just one," they must have been next to me on the couch. Junk food has certainly earned its title, but it is another temptation so many of us cannot say no to. I used to be able to eat chips by the bag. Along with the chips, I would change it up a bit once in a while and throw in corn chips and pork rinds washed down with a bottle of soda. The idea of swapping out chips for a carrot stick sounded like a good idea; putting that application to practice was another story.

If you like to snack at night your choices need to be different. The chips, leftover pizza, cookies, and cakes are very poor choices. Not only are these high in fat and low in nutrition, but as you sleep this is what your body is digesting. This junk food combo platter is not only putting on pounds, it is interfering with you getting proper sleep.

Try substituting the junk food and reach instead for carrot and celery sticks, watermelon, or cottage cheese. Fresh-popped popcorn without salt and butter, is also a good choice.

Soda Is Not Water

We can live without food for about a month, but without water we will die in less than five days. We are about 70 percent water and water is involved in every bodily function. Many overweight people drink large amounts of soda, or have been tricked into the belief that diet soda is somehow a safe substitute. If you drink a lot of soft drinks, even diet soft drinks, I would urge you to read up on Aspartame.

Aspartame has been at the forefront of controversy because of its supposed link to brain tumors, lupus, lymphoma, memory loss, ADD, diabetes, chronic fatigue, depression and multiple sclerosis type symptoms. It also has brought more complaints to the FDA than any other additive in its history. Experts also believe Aspartame makes you crave carbohydrates and increases your blood sugar levels. Sugar releases insulin into our bodies that converts to fat—the fat we see around the waist.

Although the FDA has not found evidence or determined any specific symptoms can be directly attributed to Aspartame, I would eliminate or enjoy sparingly anything with Aspartame listed as an ingredient. Drink water, water and more water, especially with a meal to aid in digestion.

Course of Action

1. **Eat at Home More.** I know life can become hectic and we must decide on taking the time to create a nice healthy salad or calling the local pizza joint and having a greasy pie delivered. We usually choose the path of least resistance and that means a pizza is on the way.

Eating out in restaurants is fine as long as it's treated as a reward. I estimate some people eat outside of the home an average of seven times a week, and that may be a conservative estimate. By preparing meals at home we know exactly what is in the foods we prepare. The amount of salt and other added chemicals can be controlled by you. Things like MSG can be eliminated if you prepare food yourself.

MSG is generally found in soup, chips, condiments, frozen dinners, salad dressings, and restaurant food. Its purpose is to enhance the flavor of food but it has been scientifically proven to cause obesity and is an addictive substance. It is not a health food and has been linked to diabetes, migraines, headaches, ADHD, and Alzheimer's. I would try and eliminate it from your diet or start requesting your meals at your favorite restaurant be prepared without it.

2. Educate Yourself. While watching people in grocery stores, I have noticed that the goal for most is to get in and get out. If people would take a few minutes to read the labels on the products they buy, a lot of these items would never leave the shelves for two reasons:

    a. You would see these products are not good to eat.

    b. You would realize they have so many preservatives that they could last on the shelves until the next millennium. So really get yourself into the habit of reading before buying, and that will make a huge difference in what you eat.

3. Do Not Eat Until You Are Full. Weight loss or weight maintenance should be a part of our everyday routine. When eating, make sure you enjoy your meal; when you are finished you should feel comfortable and ambulatory—not completely stuffed like it was a Thanksgiving dinner.

So there you have it, some sound ideas on how we should eat to maintain good health. Really no new revelations to report; I'm just asking you to remember and think about what you do, and what you need to do.

Our Idea of Entertainment

Every day you may make progress. Every step may be fruitful.
Yet there will stretch out before you an ever-lengthening, ever-ascending,
ever-improving path. You know you will never get to the end of the journey.
But this, so far from discouraging, only adds to the joy and glory of the climb.
—SIR WINSTON CHURCHILL (1874–1965)
BRITISH POLITICIAN

For a period in my life I worked as a residential contractor. It is kind of funny how we decide early on what our life's work is going to be, only to have that shift into what has been designed for us.

On one particular morning, my crew and I had a small job assigned to us in a nearby suburban neighborhood. We arrived at the home around 8:30 in the morning and then began to set up our equipment. The homeowner came into the room to see how we were doing and asked how long did we feel this project was going to take? As I started to answer, I was interrupted by a voice beckoning in the next room. "Hey everybody, come on, Springer is starting!"

Not being overly familiar with Mr. Springer's work, I became uniquely curious and followed everyone into the family room. I was invited by the six people huddled around the television to grab a cup of coffee and sit with them to watch the program. These were the same people who, fifteen minutes earlier, were asking me how long this project was going to take. Somehow the "Power of Springer" had superceded and now I was invited to take an hour off for this all-important program.

Tragedy Television

The show started out, as most talk shows do, with the host welcoming his audience and an announcement about the topic of the day. This particular show dealt with marital infidelity and how it gnaws away at a family's foundation. The host invited his guests to come on stage and sit semi-circle. Before they even had a chance to grab a chair, and seemingly without provocation, two women immediately started to attack each other. One began ripping the other's clothing and throwing punches. The other began taunting and screaming obscenities as she deflected the flailing fists.

The stagehands, after deciding that was about enough "entertainment," stepped in to separate the two female gladiators. At the same time the combatants were being ushered to their seats, the studio audience began yelling and offering each other high fives.

After some encouragement by the host to settle down, the women are finally introduced to the fired-up crowd and the man these women are competing over is seated between the two. With a prosecuting demeanor, Mr. Springer starts interrogating the guests with

148

questions; hard-hitting stuff like, "don't you know you're married?" "Do you think what you're doing is wrong?" "Hey Buddy, between you and me, which of these women do you really want to be with?"

Come On Down

As the man of the moment begins to profess his unyielding love to one, the carnage starts all over again and eventually the combatants are led off to cool down, while a new set of "victims" is escorted to the center stage. Guests are questioned and derided until the final segment of the show. After returning from a commercial break, all the show's guests are brought out and seated next to each other. You would have hoped for the problem-solving part of the program.

The moderator, however, meanders out into the studio audience and invites them to share their thoughts and feelings with everyone watching about the show's participants. Instead of getting the help they so desperately need, once again insults start flying, the crowd gets whipped up into a frenzy, and you guessed it—fists start flying once again.

The end of this debauchery comes when we get to Springer's final thoughts. Like Moses coming down from on high, ol' Jer tries to offer his perspective on what it was we just witnessed. A message he claims we can all use as a learning tool. After his brief sermon, he closes out with the words, "Take care of you and yours." Springer then walks off stage to leave the guests, like Humpty Dumpty, to put their lives back together again.

Never before have I witnessed such degrading programming. People were dehumanized at every turn and this dehumanization passes today as "entertainment." Truly we are a society obsessed with low source programming, both in television and in print. If it lacks a good balance of sex, murder, or mayhem, many of us unfortunately would choose not to watch.

The good TV "talk shows," at least in much of the public's eyes, are the ones that grab our attention and don't let go. In the quest for ratings, and because many producers work under the motto "if it bleeds, it leads," these shows typically have little regard for human decency.

A Date with Destiny

On March 5, 1995, Jonathan Schmitz was on his way to Chicago for a taping of *The Jenny Jones Show*. Mr. Schmitz was contacted by the producers of the show, asking him to appear as a guest. What the show failed to tell him was the "real" reason he was asked to appear; in fact, the show participation form he signed made no reference at all regarding the subject matter.

So how did Mr. Schmitz end up in the position of being a guest on this show? A female friend of Mr. Schmitz, Donna Riley, thought it would be a good idea to contact the show on behalf of the person who had a crush on Mr. Schmitz. The show's producers basically used her to mislead Mr. Schmitz into believing the admirer was possibly a woman he worked with, or his real hope, the woman he at one time thought he was going to marry.

The admirer ended up being a male acquaintance of Ms. Riley named Scott Amedure. During the taping of the show, Mr. Amedure went into graphic description of how he fantasized about an encounter with Schmitz, who in his words was a heterosexual. During the show, Mr. Schmitz was visibly confused and did his best to laugh it off. He was being humiliated in front of a studio audience and, if the show had aired, would have been on national television.

This was clearly the objective—to get him on the show at any cost and get a good laugh at his expense—all without regard to the effect on Mr. Schmitz. The full affect of the show was realized on March 9th when Jonathan Schmitz went to Scott Amedure's home, shooting him twice in the chest with a 12-gauge shotgun. "He f***ed me on national TV. I just walked into his house and killed him." These are the words Mr. Schmitz spoke to a 911 operator a few short minutes following Scott Amadure's death.

So what was accomplished in the name of entertainment that day? Scott Amedure lost his life at the age of 32. Jonathan Schmitz was convicted of second degree murder and is serving 25 to 50 years in a Michigan prison. Donna Riley must live everyday knowing her role in this ended one life and destroyed another. Not exactly the episode of slap-stick comedy the producers of the show were hoping for.

The New Circus

Over the last few years we have watched legitimate newsmen and women jump the fence into ambush television. One of the prime examples is Maury Povich. Mo-Po carved his initials in this programming venue by embarrassing young women searching for the father of their children. The method of proof would be determined by paternity tests—the results of which would be announced live on television.

Here is how it worked. You had the mother and the cadre of suspected fathers all seated on a stage next to each other. You let them go back and forth yelling, screaming, and accusing each other about all the reasons they were, or were not, the responsible party. You let a little animosity build and fire up the crowd, much like the Springer circus.

Once the crowd was sufficiently riled up and the accusers had made their case, an envelope would be held up containing the test results. Before the results were revealed, an obligatory commercial let even more anticipation build. Once back, it was result time. The ringleader opened the envelope, teased the crowd for about ten seconds, and announced the "winner."

A person who only moments ago was childless is now a proud parent allowed to jump from their seat, and get within inches of the other person to point fingers and speak horribly degrading words to the loser. When the person is shamed to tears, the ringleader steps in to console the mutilated soul.

I call the hosts of these shows ringleaders, and the programs they host, freak shows, because that's what they remind me of, the freak show. You remember the freak show—human beings with abnormalities, physical or mental defects, paraded around a stage for the amusement of others.

The bottom line is this live exhibition is purely dehumanizing and carries no place in a spiritual soul. There should never be a correlation between entertainment and human tragedy.

Media Madness

Recently, there was a situation where three inmates decided to leave prison without permission, and were running loose in a local neighborhood. The local anchors broke into scheduled programming with the information that referenced three escaped criminals and added details would be made available at five o'clock. *I don't know about you, but when three desperate criminals could be potentially strolling around the neighborhood, I would have preferred to know right away!*

When the five o'clock news finally airs, the stoic anchor chides, "Our top story—three escaped fugitives . . . but first a story you will hear only here on this station" and, of course, it is a story everyone is reporting on and not as important as the misplaced criminals who could be hiding in your backyard.

From the moment we wake up each morning we are bombarded with low source information—crime, pornography, advertising, corporate scandals, government fraud, the war on terror, soaring gas prices, sagging housing markets, and on, and on. It never seems to end and it is rarely spiritually uplifting. Each media outlet tries to outdo the other with "exclusives."

For goodness sake, even the weather people compete about whose Doppler radar is better. One station has Doppler 10,000, the other has Doppler 10,000 with enhanced 3D, and the third station has Doppler 10,000 with enhanced 3D with glucosamine and chondroitin.

Let's be honest, even with Doppler 50,000 and the most powerful computers known to man, the best way to forecast the weather is to simply open a window. The weather person often says, they cannot remember when the weather was so unpredictable—probably the year before would be a good guess.

Have Microphone, Will Travel

It's not enough to just report on the gloom and doom (which has a real negative effect on our disposition), the media feels we wouldn't be able at sleep at night without seeing it as well—kind of the next best thing to actually being there.

Apparently it is vital to the story to get a microphone in the face of a person who has just suffered a catastrophic loss for the purpose of "getting a feel of the story." It is not enough to know a person died in some tragic accident, we need to stick a microphone in the face of the next of kin and have a reporter hammer away with questions until they bleed with emotion into your living room.

In 2008 a case which drew national attention was the trial of Stephen Grant. Mr. Grant killed his wife Tara and then dismembered her corpse. When the legal process concluded, Stephen Grant was convicted of second degree murder. A room was set up for comments and interviews with prosecutors, attorneys, family members, and the jurors, who declined to comment.

A note written by one of the twelve jurors cited exhaustion, trauma, and a need to be left alone with their families as the reason they chose not to speak to the media and asked their anonymity be kept intact. "We would appreciate that you respect our privacy and allow us to return to being regular citizens," the note ended.

Almost immediately following that press conference, a reporter was standing on the sidewalk holding a piece of paper into the camera stating he had an "exclusive." "What I am holding, are the names of the jurors who sat on the Stephen Grant murder trial . . . and our news station was the only station able to obtain this list."

The next thing we see is a teary-eyed, visibly shaken woman who was one of the jurors staring into a camera, blinding light in her eyes, and this reporter doing exactly what he was asked to refrain from. I understand there is freedom *of* the press, but there should also be freedom *from* the press, and a right to privacy.

Get Granny Her Reading Glasses

When I was a kid, once a week my Grandma would ask me to walk to the store to buy her "little papers" as she called them. Grandpa called them the scandal sheets—today we call them tabloid trash. On the cover of one of these little papers was a kangaroo with a human infant in the pouch, and she told me she was convinced this was actual, truthful journalism.

It was funny, and kind of cute, but fast-forward to today in any grocery store checkout lane in the country. I would challenge you to find a magazine that does not have a story about Brittany, Lindsey, Nicole, or Paris. Digging up dirt on celebrities, showing them in the weakest of states, is what sells magazines today. But there is no value in human suffering, period—no matter whom it is written about.

Thanks for Caring

It has been a while now since the big tabloid news involved Brad Pitt, Angelina Jolie, and Jennifer Anniston. But there was a time when their story was splashed over the pages of every tabloid in every grocery store. People apparently just couldn't get enough of the "Brangelina" stuff and how poor Jennifer was being left at the curbside.

When I am in a store where this stuff is sold, I will occasionally pick up a magazine. I do not pick it up because I enjoy the articles, or have the urge to get caught up on what is happening in "Holly-weird." Nor do I need to keep up on the latest fashion trends or latest diet craze. What I do look for are the Letters to the Editor.

Letters are published from all across the country from ordinary working-class people wanting these multi-millionaire celebrities to know they are loved and supported. They are encouraged by the writers to not pay attention to what has been written about their trysts and that they are there to support them.

By writing this letter, what is the expectation? As Brad sips his latte, he stumbles across the letter, leans over to Angelina, and says, "Wow, I just read a letter from Helen in Peoria; she says not to worry about all of the stuff they are writing about us." "Sure is nice of Helen." "Ang, you need to have her over for brunch, so we can thank her."

I hate to be the bearer of bad news, but these people you want to somehow align your life with could not care less about you, nor one aspect of your life—good or bad. Writing letters of support will in no way improve the quality of your life.

The Forgiven

We are a forgiving society for sure. We are always willing to give people the benefit of a second chance after all. Think about your own life for a moment—*how many chances has God given you?* My question is who do we forgive, and not forgive? We want to forgive the preacher, the celebrity, the athlete juiced up on steroids, but rarely, if ever, do we forgive the person we sleep and wake with; the person we walk this long and difficult journey with.

I think what it boils down to is that we are able to forgive those we have an unattached admiration for, but those we are personally involved, attached, and close with, are much more susceptible to our human side. Remember that you can only be in one place at any given time, and those around you are far greater in terms of importance, in terms of growth, because God put them there for a reason. Our purpose is to nurture these people, and walk with them to their realized purpose.

It is not my intention to insult or question what you have found to be entertaining or what you choose to read. I just want you to

157

think about how we associate importance in our lives. As much as I enjoy watching reruns of *The A-Team*, it's still not as important as the people in my life.

I implore you to stay informed, stay abreast of what is going on in your community, state, and our world. When you come across a story on television that represents low source information, I would suggest you pass. I would also recommend you save the four dollars on the trashy magazines and keep your life as positive as possible.

Focus your energies on the good things in this world, even though you may have to dig deep to find them. The media sells fear, and the public buys into it. Let those laugh at you because you are different, but know you can laugh back, because they are all the same.

~

Wedding Gifts

We all have daily rituals. From the moment we wake, they begin. Making the bed, showering, getting dressed, fixing breakfast—all day we have mundane routines and tasks we need to accomplish. To end this book, *which I pray you found helpful,* I have added seven additional tasks you should implement into your life. If practiced on a daily basis, they will make a difference in your life for the better— they did in mine.

1. **Steer Clear of Opinions and Judgments.** Far too many of us go through our day consumed by what others think and say. What may be worse, however, is how we react to these situations. I say, *"react"* because reacting is a low source word. Responding positively, rather than reacting negatively, is more resourceful given most situations. We get so caught up with the need to be liked and accepted

by every person we encounter, it becomes counterproductive. Thinking every person we meet will like us is not realistic.

I have personal knowledge of a person afflicted with this need—a never-ending desire to be liked by everyone. If this person feels the people surrounding them are "not on their side," they put up an automatic defense mechanism.

It is their way of throwing insecurity onto everyone around them. They have a constant, seemingly never-ending quest for approval and have developed a habit of asking advice as to what is needed to gain that approval. In reality, the only place one can go to answer that question is inside oneself. Because, as is usually the case, the advice you receive from others is usually not the advice you needed to hear.

Charles Barkley was once asked during a promotional tour for his best selling book, *I May Be Wrong, But I Doubt It* (Random House, 2003), how he handled what people thought about him. Charles said simply, "You go by the fifty-fifty rule; half are going to be with you and the other half won't." It is simply a matter of managing your thoughts, which leads to managing your life, regardless of what half of the people might say or think.

I remember standing in the lobby following my very first lecture. Most of the people who approached me came by to discuss how much they enjoyed the lecture and how inspired they were about what they had heard. Being new at this, I was feeling pretty good about myself, glad that I was able to reach so many people with my message.

As I wrapped up one conversation, I noticed a woman standing about ten feet away. I could tell she had something on her mind and she finally summoned the courage to approach me. She shook my hand, and to my surprise, stated bluntly that after the thirty-minute lecture she had come away with absolutely nothing of value. Being new to the lecture circuit and wanting to make an impression on everyone, I asked her what she thought I needed to do to improve.

What just happened here? Instead of keeping my attention on all of the positive things people were sharing with me, I completely shifted my attention to the one person who decided to offer up a little criticism. At this stage of my life, I realized that if I were to keep changing what I write and the topics I lecture on, nothing would come from me—it would be from the voices of those I felt I needed to impress.

I understand the need to make a good impression; I understand that at times we seek the advice of those we respect. All I am saying is to follow your heart, do what is right for your life, and what makes the most sense for you. Do not do things just because you think others will approve, and do not go out of your way to impress those who criticize. Unless it is advice or constructive criticism you seek from others, and feel they are worth listening to, do not compromise your beliefs.

2. Balance Your Boundaries with the Word "No." This **Wedding Gift** is similar to the first in the sense that when we are in the approval-seeking mode, the word **no** is rarely given as an answer. Is it possible to give into every demand that is placed on us? Not a chance. We all want to do everything we can for those around us. It is human nature just to say "yes." Yet there are times we overwhelm ourselves with commitments, rather than simply saying, "I'm sorry, but I just cannot right now."

What we need to remember is that our decision-making process is reached at a conscious level. Our gut instinct is to cave into the pressure of saying "yes" to the person asking because we feel indebted to them in one way or another. In the back of our mind, we feel we owe them something due to a favor or act of kindness they did for us at one time in our lives. Believe me when I tell you that once you cave into the request, there will always be another request.

It is a great feeling to be the one that "can be counted on," but every time you say "yes" when you really meant "no," a little resentment will build internally. Simply by saying, "I am sorry, but I just cannot at this time," will free you from unnecessary low source commitments.

3. Let Happiness Find You. Happiness is not a transient state, and the ways we are led to believe where true happiness can be found, in the end, have been proven false. We pack up and move onto the next experience, searching for something we may never find. One of the greatest ironies about happiness is that those who find it are usually those who spend no time chasing it. Nathaniel Hawthorne said it best. "Happiness is as a butterfly which, when pursued, is always beyond our grasp, but which, if you will sit down quietly, may alight upon you." Ultimately, those who receive happiness seem the least interested in finding it.

Here is an example: I have a friend who believes his path to happiness is to be in a loving relationship, which when you think about it is admirable. *I do not know many people who would choose isolation over love.* His pursuit takes him to weekly singles dances and to Internet dating sites. Every Monday he has met someone who is, of course, *"The One,"* but by Wednesday reality sets in, and on Friday, it is back to the chase.

This constant pursuit eventually brings us back to the same place, because happiness is not a commodity—it is a natural state of being. Once we commit to decreasing our pursuit to find it, we automatically increase the absolute certainty it will show up at our door.

4. Learn to Slow Down. Mahatma Gandhi once said, "There is more to life than increasing its speed." This is especially true for those of us in here in the West.

About a year ago, I spent ten days at a resort in the Caribbean—January in Michigan is the perfect time to get away to a tropical climate. As I was standing in line to check in at the resort, it became obvious to me which tourists were Americans and which were from other countries. I also remember being impressed with the resort staff; their attention to detail was admirable, but if your idea of good service involved speed, well, you had definitely come to the wrong place.

The American tourists began to get fidgety, looking at their watches, sighing, and putting their hands on their hips. *I know because I was one of them.* There was one man in line who began ranting in rather colorful language, invoking expletives with God's name, demanding to speak with the manager. He was irritated that he had been in line for a grand total of fifteen minutes. The slogan of the Jamaican people apparently is "What is your rush, man?"

After becoming friendly with the staff, I began to ask questions about life on the island, and here is what I came away with—the Jamaican people take life a little slower than people in most cultures, and spirituality is very important to them. Heart disease and cancer are not as common as in other parts of the world, because of the slower pace and lack of stress. "Hurry, worry, and scurry" are not built into the fabric of the people of Jamaica.

These people, like many cultures, do not measure every activity in terms of speed. They have a laid-back style that suits them well, and you know what? It is okay to slow down occasionally.

In the West, we hear all the time that stress is the main cause of many of our ailments. We worry ourselves to the point of needing medication just to deal with life. Think about where we came from— a place of joy, peace, calmness, and patience. Yet we tend to see every situation in our lives as emergencies that need to be taken care of at lightning speed. When this happens, we miss so much of the beauty and splendor that surrounds us.

5. Live Life Without Regret. Regret is ultimately about all of the things we failed to do. I have a lot of regret in my life, and people around me make sure I do not forget it. When you see yourself for who you truly are, the way you see yourself matches what you see as well. I think we can all remember a time when we uttered words that we wish we could take back.

The great Hindu philosopher Krishnamurti once said, "Without freedom from the past, there is no freedom at all, because the mind is never new, fresh, innocent." For some, you forgive unconditionally, and this is true forgiveness. For others, you forgive with the caveat of the constant reminder. You are told that you are forgiven, but the forgiver is always right there to remind you of the fact. This is not forgiveness.

True forgiveness is a one-time thing. You give it and never return to the incident. I believe people do the best they can with what is available to them. *I know this to be true based on where I was, and the person I am today.* I do not see regret associated with guilt or shame. Holding yourself hostage by personal guilt or shame is one of the greatest paths to self-destruction, because of the ways we try to mask the guilt and shame.

Pretend you are wearing an empty backpack. As you go through life, you add a brick to the pack for each incident that caused you regret. At some point, the weight will become too great and consequently you will not be able to move forward anymore. That is what regret does—it weighs you down.

When I think about the things that I regret most in life, the ones that hurt the most are the times I failed to live in the moment. I think about the opportunities I missed because I failed to act, or failed to be there when I was needed the most. This is really what regret is—failure to act when it was most important.

Someone once said, "Life is a series of moments; string as many good ones together as possible." Moving forward, thinking from your true self, and risking without fear of failure and rejection are the way to live a regret-free life. As I said this earlier in the book, when we are at the end of the physical part of life, our focus will not be on the credit card companies we owe money to, or the work we have not completed. Our focus will be on regret: the things we had a chance to do or say, the actions we did not implement, or the words we held back.

6. Give Your Body What It Needs. Your body is designed and created by God for this physical journey—your body is sacred. For an assortment of reasons or excuses, we took on a belief that filling our bodies with toxins and poisons was an acceptable thing to do. Giving our body what it needs does not mean we fill our lungs with cigarette smoke, inject our blood stream with narcotics, or consume excess alcohol. It means treating your body in the manner it was intended to be treated.

Our bodies are exactly the way God intended them to be—no mistakes, flaws, or blemishes, but unfortunately, most people do not see it that way. In order for us to be happy, many of us feel the need to alter its appearance and find escape through drugs and alcohol. These are notions that all provide false positives in the real world. The external world has nothing of value when it comes to comfort and tranquility. It is high time to realize that it is okay to be comfortable in the skin you were born with.

Exercise and nutrition are key elements in giving the body what it so desperately needs. As for proper maintenance for our bodies, I am more of a student than teacher. I have learned a great deal from fitness experts at my local gym, where you will find me twice a day. When I went for my initial assessment, I soon realized how much I had mistreated my body. I was overweight and out-of-shape, but fortunately not to the point of it being hopeless to make positive changes.

Once you begin to feel the effects of a sensible exercise program, it quickly becomes a part of your every day life—one of your daily rituals. If you live near a fitness facility and are thinking about making a lifestyle change, I would highly recommend a visit. If you are not interested in joining a club, there are a lot of alternative activities you can do to get your heart rate up and your body in shape. Sports, gardening, dancing, or just plain old-fashioned walking are a few examples. Find something that works for you—and stick with it. Results do not happen overnight, and it takes thirty days for a routine to become a habit. However, the results of replacing the old with the new are worth it.

7. Take Out the Trash. In every home, there is a receptacle where we place the trash that accumulates throughout the day; food we cannot run through the disposal, newspapers, junk mail, and so on. If we fail to empty the receptacle, it begins to leave an odor. If allowed to linger, it will ultimately become a health risk.

The same concept holds true with our minds. Each day has the potential of bringing situations that create havoc in our lives, and if allowed to fester, have the potential to cause us problems as well. A bad morning commute, a computer that crashes, an unrealistic deadline at work, or the children becoming unruly are some examples.

If these situations in our daily routine are allowed to accumulate, they will manifest into counterproductive behavior and ultimately a health risk. At some point before going to bed, you need to empty the mental trash of the day, preferably right before you go to sleep. Find a quiet place, close your eyes, put your mind on cruise control, and empty all of that negative energy.

Do this little exercise for ten to fifteen minutes a night, and make it an evening ritual. I especially like to do this exercise in the backyard, just before sunset on a warm summer evening. Make a point to connect with the beauty all around you.

Just Do It

I have had a number of people tell me that all of this advice sure sounds nice, but they just cannot find the time to put any of it into practice. That is nothing more than an excuse for people who are not willing to take the time to do what is necessary to improve their overall health and well-being.

Steer clear of opinions and judgments, balance your boundaries with the word "no," let happiness find you, learn to slow down, live life without regret, give your body what it needs, and remember to take out the trash. Implement these seven gifts into your life and you will be amazed at the positive benefits you will gain. These are independent tasks which are simple to do, but when combined together will bring enormous joy, focus, and direction into your life.

∾

Conclusion

Talent does what it can, genius does what it must.
—ROBERT BULWER-LYTTON (1831–91)
ENGLISH STATESMAN AND POET

If at any point I came across as controversial or challenged your belief system, then I believe I have accomplished what God wanted me to. The personal growth and spiritual awakening that took place in my life is available to everyone. I just hope and pray, that in some small way, I helped you realize that the journey is available to you as well.

God wants all of us to dream big, play big, and live big. He also wants us to accept the challenges, pain, and difficulties in life, as well as embrace the good we receive. Transformation requires us to do a little work, but it is not about learning anything new, it is all about remembering our spiritual beginnings.

Living life based on spiritual principles does not exclude you from the pains this existence will bring. What it does offer is this— a superior way to handle those challenges, and an ability to catch ourselves when the ego takes over the heart and mind.

If you are familiar with my work, the idea of conforming and falling in line is not a prescription I encourage you to fill. *Live your life with passion and with purpose.* Stand up for what you believe in, be considerate of others, and most importantly, take the time to *talk less* and *listen more.*

May God love you,
Paul Wedding